Why Now

How Good Timing Makes Great Products

By Paul Orlando

To my lovely wife, Susan Joan.

What Is the Why Now Question and Why Is It Important?   6

    How We Ask the Question   7

    This Book Is for Founders, Product Team Members, Early Hires, and Investors   8

    How Others Think About the Why Now Question   10

Introducing the Timing Drivers   15

Introducing the Why Now Session   17

    Timing Advantages Require an Improved, Sustainable Business Model   18

Case Study: YouTube's Why Now   20

After the Why Now Session   30

    Challenging the Session   30

    Rework After the Challenge   32

    Avoid the Analysis of Others   33

    Don't Do This: Running a Bad Why Now Session   38

    Don't Do This: Running a Bad Challenge Session   39

Timing Drivers   42

    Technology: Performance Curves   43

    Social/Behavioral: The Enduring Human Condition, Fads, and More   45

    Regulatory/Legal: Prohibitions and Requirements   47

    Installed Base: Existing Devices or Systems   49

    Crisis: The Wildcard   51

    Economic: Ups and Downs   52

    Networks: Connections and Flows   53

    Distribution: Reaching Your Customers and Resources   54

    Capital Access: Funding, Investment Appetite, and Options   55

    Organizational: Risk, Efficiency, and Learning   56

Available Talent: The Builders 58

Demographic: Predictable and Projected 59

The Problem with Solving Problems 60

Mistaking Capability for Desirability 64

Mistaking Lack of the Product for the Lack of the Person 65

Mistaking Lack of the Business for the Lack of the Capability 66

Timing Considerations 68

Competitive Effects 68

About First-Mover Advantage 69

Matching What Won't Change With What Is Changing 70

Investors and Why Now 72

Why Now Slides In Pitch Decks 75

How Early Should You Invest? 77

When Previous Bad Experience Means Ignoring Second Chances 78

How Early Should You Build? 79

Timing Shifts the Market Size 81

Too Early Examples 84

Timing in Different Markets 86

Your Market Type Impacts Your Timing Advantage 86

In a Gold Rush Should You Sell Shovels? 91

When a Timing Advantage Requires an Ecosystem 92

Timing Brakes and Blockers 94

Timing Patterns 99

The Hermit Crab 99

The Unlocked Asset 100

The New Capability 100

The Predictable 101

The New Freedom   101

The Clone   102

The Toy   103

The Removed Barrier   104

The System Shock   104

The Unavoidable   105

The Moral Urgency   105

The Psychological Barrier   106

The Analog to Digital   107

Bad Patterns   110

The Wrong Curve   111

The Oversold Utopia   113

The Illusion of Immediacy   114

Does Focusing on Timing Devalue Founders?   116

Execution Risk vs Market Risk   117

Steam-Engine Time   119

Summing Up   123

Appendixes   125

Running the Why Now Session   125

Business Model Impact   127

Evaluating Your Why Now   128

Questions to Ask About Timing Drivers   131

If You Have No Strong Timing Advantage   134

Bibliography   136

Thank You   138

Endnotes   140

What Is the Why Now Question and Why Is It Important?

Have you had this experience?

You come up with an idea and work to make it happen. It fails. Then years later, you see another similar idea pop up and succeed. Frustrating.

But you have the consolation of being able to say: "I thought of it first! I was just too early."

If not you, maybe you know someone else who went through all that. If not someone else you know, then you've probably heard similar examples in the news.

Whether it's you, your friends, or others you've heard about, being first (but too early) is a sorry consolation for being right on time.

Being too early is just a polite way of saying you were wrong.

. . . .

Deciding what product or business to build depends on many things. The problem you're trying to solve, the size of the opportunity, your capabilities, what you're passionate about, people involved, how much time you have, your budget, and even temporary considerations like current trends and availability of funding.

You have other questions if you're evaluating potential investments. Or if you're a startup founder or an early team member. Or even if you're part of a team in a larger organization developing new products in-house.

Where should you focus your limited time and resources? Part of that decision comes down to wanting to focus on the opportunities most likely to succeed.

Many things influence your likelihood of success, but there is one factor we recognize as important, even if few seem to really dive into how it works. That's the importance of timing, often called the "why now" question.

The why now question has become common in the startup world but is relevant in many situations.

How We Ask the Question

Depending on your focus, the why now question itself can take different forms.

- "Why is this the right time to build this product or business?" What bigger forces support this type of product or business becoming a success? Are we pursuing new inventions that are years from becoming business model-supported innovations with customers?

- "Does the market environment give this product or business an advantage?" What is the mix of potential customers and businesses that could serve those customers? How does that environment give this product or business an advantage or disadvantage?

- "As a potential investor or early employee, should I wait to see how things develop before going in? Do I risk being too early if I invest or join now? Are companies generally at more of an advantage if they enter early or late? How could I evaluate whether the timing is right for us?"

These questions look simple. But as with many simple questions, there's a lot going on. And it takes a while to uncover the answers.

In this book, I've collected a variety of options and practical recommendations to help you implement them. You'll also find many examples that you can refer to, making it simpler to relate to your unique circumstances.

Because we're dealing with the question of timing, I include what I call timing diagrams with those examples as a way to visualize how timing can end up becoming favorable (or not).

Here's a very basic visualization as an introduction. The horizontal X-axis is time.

The basic ideas are 1) there is more risk being too early than too late, 2) something external to the company creates an opportunity during the middle phase when the market window opens, and 3) late entrants can still succeed by entering a niche.

I'll return to this diagram with more detail as we build our understanding of timing.

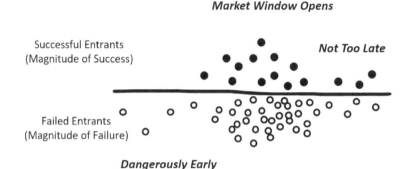

Before I forget: feel free to say hello at paul@StartupsUnplugged.com or find me on LinkedIn. I'll post updates there. If you want access to more of the data that I used for this book, visit StartupsUnplugged.com.

This Book Is for Founders, Product Team Members, Early Hires, and Investors

Over the years I've seen a lot of change in the way people build businesses, especially startups.

Many large companies also adopted these changes. Some of the work I do with larger organizations is specifically to help them act more like startups. That is, the fast-moving part, not the high failure-rate part.

Years ago, it was rare to see startup founders systematically go out to learn from their potential customers before building a product. And then, once those same founders learned a bit, it was also rare to see them build something minimal to test and learn if they were on the right track, before committing to build even more. Thanks to books like *Four Steps to the Epiphany*, *The Lean Startup,* and *Business Model Innovation*, methodologies like Jobs To Be Done and concepts like the minimum viable product, lots of off-the-shelf tools and entrepreneurial education, many people changed the way they learn from customers and build products.

It's time we do the same for the question of timing.

This book is especially for you if you fit into one of these categories:

- You're a startup founder, working to understand how your company may be at an advantage because of timing. How should you highlight that advantage when raising funding? Or when you hire talent, how could you describe how big your business could grow?

- You're part of a product team within a larger organization. What timing considerations should guide your new product development? How could you use an evaluation of timing to help acquire a budget and generate internal support for your work? You may have many internal concepts, but you can't run with all of them. How do you filter opportunities and choose the most promising ones? How could you identify new opportunities using timing analysis?

- You're a potential early hire and want to join a team working on strong opportunities. If you join industries and companies with a good chance to grow, your own opportunities will grow too. Apart from team, role, and compensation, what else should you look for?

- You invest and want to focus your system for evaluating opportunities. Where should you search for investment opportunities? What should you ignore, even if others rush in? What should you keep monitoring for later investment?

Many people agree with the advice that timing is important, but how do you use that advice?

Exploring this topic over the past few years, I found awareness of timing's importance, but also that some of the assumptions about the topic were uncharted or unhelpful. What seems to be good advice is actually not helpful unless you think about timing differently and can act on it. I will help you do that.

I also want to mention what I'm *not* writing about.

This book is not about why you personally should found or join a company. People are different. This isn't a book about finding your passion or life meaning.

Importantly, this book is not about predicting the future. Instead, it provides some ways you could put structure behind your exploration of possible futures, how you might want to participate in them, how to decide where to focus, and how to think through the impact of different scenarios.

Predicting the future is a game best played when no one keeps score. What I am trying to do is more practical. That is, what possibilities are opening up? Where could opportunity probabilistically lie? And how should we act?

Faced with multiple options, this book will help you decide.

Faced with open-ended opportunities, this book will help you identify where to play.

Faced with having to express your decision, this book will help you explain why you chose a specific path.

You'll also find many examples and exercises to practice and use your knowledge live.

The reason I'm in a good place to write this is that I've started businesses that were both too early (not much fun) and then at exactly the right time (much more fun). I've built and operated four startup accelerators and incubators around the world and have seen many startups struggle with (or often ignore) questions of timing. I've taught entrepreneurship classes at a major university with a large entrepreneurship center (the University of Southern California). I've brought the timing question into the mix as a hands-on workshop for external startups and grad students. I've also presented publicly about this topic many times while putting my thoughts together.

How Others Think About the Why Now Question

As investor and Netscape founder Marc Andreesen said: *"Track startups over multiple decades, what you find is that most ideas do end up working. It's much more a question of 'when' not 'if'…"*

Just look at a very partial list of Dotcom era startups that failed, paired with the related successes that came later. Andreesen's comment seems to hold. *The ideas themselves weren't bad if others eventually went on to succeed at building them.*

Category	Name	First Available	Active/Discontinued
Grocery delivery	Webvan	1999	Discontinued 2001
	Instacart	2012	Active
Local Delivery	Kozmo	1998	Discontinued 2001
	Postmates	2011	Active (acquired by Uber in 2020)
Social Networking	SixDegrees	1997	Discontinued 2000
	Facebook	2004	Active
Pet Products	Pets.com	1998	Discontinued 2000
	Chewy	2011	Active (acquired by PetSmart in 2017)
Fashion	Boo	1998	Discontinued 2000
	Shein	2008	Active
Music	Napster	1999	Discontinued 2002 (though later revived)
	Spotify	2006	Active
Cloud	Network Computer	1998	Discontinued 1999
	AWS	2006	Active

A very limited list of failed Dotcoms and later comparables

Or is Andreesen's comment specific to new tech companies? What about a focus on timing from history?

Let's ground ourselves by going back a couple centuries to Napoleon Bonaparte -- someone who upended entire governments in Europe. You'd think Napoleon would believe that he could do whatever he wanted, whenever he wanted, through force. And yet, in his final exile, when it came to the importance of timing he said:

"I might have conceived many plans; but I never had it in my power to execute any. I held the helm with a vigorous hand; but the fury of the waves was greater than any force I could exert in resisting them; and I prudently yielded, rather than incur the risk of sinking through stubborn opposition. I never was truly my own master; but was always controlled by circumstances." [1]

And we also have the Hollywood approach to this. *The Graduate,* an old movie about the angst of a young college grad, is known for a few famous scenes. In one scene, the graduate (Benjamin) is given career advice by his cryptic neighbor (Mr. McGuire):

> *Mr. McGuire: "I want to say one word to you. Just one word."*
>
> *Benjamin: "Yes, sir."*
>
> *Mr. McGuire: "Are you listening?"*
>
> *Benjamin: "Yes, I am."*
>
> *Mr. McGuire: "Plastics."*
>
> *Benjamin: "Exactly how do you mean?"*
>
> *Mr. McGuire: "There's a great future in plastics. Think about it. Will you think about it?"*

We laugh at that scene, but the thing is… McGuire was right. And he was talking about timing.

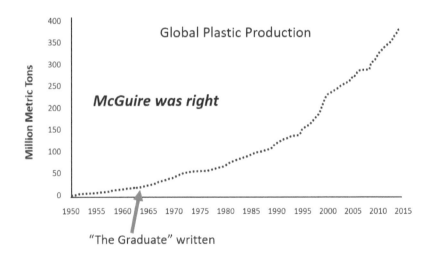

The plastics industry went on to grow at a tremendous rate after his comment. If you were a young college graduate at the time, as Benjamin was, you could have built a company or a career in the plastics industry.

Note that McGuire didn't say "go work for DuPont," or "you should join Dow Chemical." He said "plastics" and then let Benjamin sort out his path forward (which ended up not involving plastics at all).

So in this book, I'm modifying Andreesen, Napoleon, and McGuire's comments to the simple:

Understanding timing in your market is essential. When teams don't ask 'why now' they miss opportunities to be more successful and risk setting themselves up for failure.

Thinking about timing is a mix of art and science. And just because the time for something may be ripe, it doesn't mean that it will happen. That still depends upon people acting. Sometimes it just takes someone to realize that there's an opportunity. We'll discuss that as well.

You'll learn how to run a "Why Now Session" and to make timing maps to evaluate the way different drivers might impact your business' timing. For these, I provide case studies and many other examples.

For those who might reconsider their plans if they don't believe they have a timing advantage, I provide ways to think through your next best options.

Here's a quick example from a company you probably know: the short-term rental platform Airbnb.

Airbnb's own founding story is an example of apparently accidental good timing, but it didn't start out looking that way. After starting the company in 2008, Airbnb's founders received rejection after rejection from potential investors.

As one well-known investor, Fred Wilson of Union Square Ventures, recounted:

"We couldn't wrap our heads around air mattresses on living room floors as the next hotel room and did not chase the deal..."[2]

But there was, however, at least one person interested.

As angel investor Paige Craig described, he was already out looking for a virtual hotel.[3] He already had a hypothesis that called for the existence of something like Airbnb. When he found Airbnb by searching online, he reached out to the founders.

Craig's potential investment in Airbnb fell apart for unrelated reasons, but he had identified the need for something like an Airbnb and the pieces needed for it to work. From early documents, the founders themselves might not have understood the benefits of their timing – being able to solve problems of excess real estate, trust, scheduling, and payments during an economic recession – and how it impacted their eventual strength.

For Airbnb in 2008, as well as Dropbox in 2007, YouTube in 2005, Netflix in 1997, and for many more examples we'll cover in this book, those new businesses benefited from good timing.

Those businesses rode a wave of emerging opportunity. Rather than fight the fury of the waves, they yielded to the larger forces of their time.

In other examples, an existing business released a new product at the right time and rode the timing to greater success, for example Apple with the iPhone in 2007, Amazon with AWS in 2006, Motorola with the DynaTAC in 1984, and more.

But in still other examples, businesses did the opposite. They tried to build at the wrong time with no strong timing advantage or they exited just before what was to become a promising market.

As Marc Andreessen further said:

"The great irony is all the ideas of the '90s were basically correct. They were just too early. We all thought the future would happen very quickly. But instead things crashed and burned. The ideas are really just coming true now. Timing is everything. But it's also the hardest thing to control. It's hard; entrepreneurs are congenitally wired to be too early. And being too early is a bigger problem for entrepreneurs than not being correct. It's very hard to sit and just wait for things to arrive."[4]

So how do *you* identify *your* Why Now?

Introducing the Timing Drivers

The first way I look at the why now question is to identify the main drivers of timing that impact a given business.

Then we develop a perspective on how one or more of these drivers impacts your odds of success.

There are many drivers of timing advantages. They can overlap. And yes, others have looked at similar lists, but we're going to do something different with these drivers.

This is the list of drivers I detail in this book. I'll spend more time on the first five.

1. Technological: Performance curves and cost improvement (may be predictable).

2. Social/Behavioral: Trends (may be predictable or sudden, often existing in observable niches first).

3. Regulatory/Legal: Prohibitions and requirements, patents (predictable in expiry), and laws (less predictable).

4. Installed Base: Tipping points reached in users of supporting equipment and systems.

5. Crisis: Is the business coincidentally positioned to benefit or can it act quickly?

6. Economic: Growth or decline (may be quick or slow).

7. Networks: Connections enable something new.

8. Distribution: Changes the ability to reach customers.

9. Capital Access: What are the sources and what is their impact?

10. Organizational: Impact to cost of production and risk.

11. Available Talent: Who can build what we need and how do we gain access to them?

12. Demographic: Changing demand trends (may be predictable).

I'll bring out more detail on these throughout the book rather than devote lots of upfront time to each one separately.

These drivers often work together, as we'll later see.

Changing and Not Changing

So far, I've only mentioned looking at what is changing, but that's not the only approach.

Instead, Amazon founder Jeff Bezos is known to focus on what will not change. As Bezos said:

"I very frequently get the question: 'What's going to change in the next 10 years?' And that is a very interesting question; it's a very common one. I almost never get the question: 'What's not going to change in the next 10 years?'"[5]

His point was that the unchanging parts of the world offer a more stable foundation on which to build a long-term business. In Amazon's case, this meant focusing on cheaper prices and faster delivery.

But timing drivers affect those unchanging parts as well. In Amazon's case, many of the company's responses to those unchanging parts of its business came when the timing was right. We'll discuss these as demand-side and supply-side timing factors later on.

The overall processes I'll show will help you think about when to attack a changing world, or an unchanging one, problems to be solved, and new capabilities to be exploited.

In the years before I wrote this book, I would hear people mention timing as one of the important parts of a business' success, but also complain that they didn't have helpful and replicable guidance on how to figure it out.

So here it is.

Introducing the Why Now Session

I'm going to bring you through something I call a Why Now Session. This is a methodical way to determine your potential timing benefits.

If you go through this process, you'll come out with an understanding of your timing advantages, the ability to defend your position, and a way to present your reasoning.

You'll also know when timing might not be in your favor.

While you might already be looking at timing, you can run a Why Now Session for specific reasons and audiences.

- You're getting ready to raise capital and you know that a strong Why Now improves your ability to convince investors that you're a good bet. You already convinced yourselves that you're on the right track and can build something big, but you're now trying to convince someone outside of your own team.

- You're making a decision on new product development within an existing organization. You might have internal R&D and product development capabilities to build many different products. You could go in a number of directions and you want to improve your odds of choosing wisely. You need another filter on where to put resources.

- You're an investor searching for another way to reduce bias in investment decisions. How can you evaluate market readiness in a systematic way? Since there are a limited number of companies you can invest in, how can you evaluate their potential?

Whatever your reason for investigating timing, run the session with the right team.

For a small startup getting ready to raise its first round, that may be just the founders. A bit later stage, that might be the CEO, CTO, Head of Product, and more. For investors, that might be a few people on the deal team.

If you have no strong timing advantage, the Why Now Session will help you face that reality. Not having a strong timing advantage is not the end of a business, but it will change how you express what you do, including seeking advantages elsewhere.

The goal of the session is to come away with an understanding of whether a timing advantage exists and if so, a description of why that is and what you're going to do about it.

To show you how to do that I'll go through a case study where I've applied the framework. I only use a few timing drivers in this example, but it will help you understand the overall process. Later in the book I'll take you through all 12 drivers, how they work, how they combine, and more.

But one important qualifier first.

Timing Advantages Require an Improved, Sustainable Business Model

Without a new business model that is both financially sustainable and also an improvement over current examples, you have no timing advantage. Yes, there are products that only become possible to build because of tech developments, a regulatory change, or a crisis. But if there is no improved, sustainable business model those products will eventually fizzle out.

To be useful, you must note the effects of your timing drivers and outcomes of your Why Now Session and map them to your business model.

This is a step often left out when people talk about timing. They focus on the "why" and the "what," but don't take steps to understand the "when" and "how" that impacts the product's business model.

There are any number of changes that could only happen at this moment. How many of these changes impact your business model favorably?

But first, what's a standard way to define a business model?

A versatile explanation from startup author Ash Maurya is that a business model describes three things:

- The value the business creates for its customers.
- The value the business captures from its customers.
- The cost the business incurs to provide value to its customers.

Those three parts are general enough to describe the business model for any business.

Importantly, for a financially sustainable business, those three parts must differ in magnitude in the following way.

Value created for your customers	>	Value captured by the business	≥	Cost to provide the value

The leftmost item (value the business creates for its customers) must be greater than the central item (value the business captures from its customers), which in turn must be greater, or at least equal to the rightmost item (cost of providing value to its customers). Otherwise, the business is not financially sustainable.

Note that we have many examples of businesses breaking the above magnitude flow in the short term.

Raise a lot of capital and you can lose money on each customer – for a while.

Or seek market share and you can choose to lose money – for a while.

Or be subsidized by another part of the business – for a while.

But eventually, the business needs to respect that flow like a law of nature.

(If you want to dig into the business model topic, check out an earlier book I wrote called *Growth Units*.)

Here's an example with a large, successful company to gain more familiarity with the Why Now Session and business model process.

Case Study: YouTube's Why Now

Whenever I read about a process, I wish there were examples to help take me through them. I feel like I only really understand what to do once I see it in action. So if you're like me in that respect, this next section is for you.

I'm going to stick with YouTube, which launched in 2005, to demonstrate the above technique.

The following info is from both the "Viacom vs Google (YouTube)" lawsuit that exposed Sequoia's investment memo and other research on the companies and technologies mentioned.[6]

1) Scanning the list of timing drivers, these look like the most important for YouTube when it launched and raised money in 2005.

Most Relevant Drivers	Relevant History (Make a list of earlier attempts that didn't work and why. Or earlier attempts that did work, but in a limited or different way. Include dates.)	Future expectations (Depends on driver type and expected speed of change. Include expected dates.)
Technology: Moore's Law (the number of transistors on a microchip doubles approximately every two years, meaning that computation becomes faster and cheaper over time)	Falling cost of data storage needed for video files. Cost of storage for typical short videos (only 7 Megs at the time) was less than $0.01 in 2005.	Expected to continue to decline. Data storage cost projections are available.

Technology: Edholm's Law (bandwidth of telecommunications networks doubles approximately every 18 months)	Increasing data speeds for streaming large video files. By 2005 it was already common for people to have broadband in the home. Broadband to the home grew at over 30% per year in the lead up to 2005, with approximately 50% of US households having broadband by 2005. Cost of bandwidth for typical short video files was less than $0.01 in 2005.	Expected to continue to decline. Projected along Edholm's Law curve.
Social/Behavioral	More people are comfortable with sharing images and videos and videoing themselves. Relevant acquisitions: Picasa (digital photo organizing service launched in 2002) was acquired by Google in 2004, Snapfish (online photo sharing and printing) was acquired by HP in 2005, and Flickr (photo sharing site launched in early 2004) was acquired by Yahoo! in 2005.	Expected to continue. People will not stop sharing online as it becomes easier to do so. People already sharing images will start to share video.
Social/Behavioral	Social networking sites like MySpace, Friendster, LinkedIn, and Facebook launched in 2003 and 2004 and are growing in popularity.	Expected to continue. These social networking sites will drive both supply and demand of online video.
Installed Base	Webcams connected to a computer became common with annual sales in the tens of millions of units sold by 2005.	Expected to become more popular as they become cheaper and better.

Installed Base	Digital cameras (can be carried around and then connected to a computer to upload files) unit shipments were approximately 60M in 2004 and 65M in 2005, globally.	Expected to become more popular as they become cheaper and better.
Regulatory/Legal	*Problems distributing copyrighted content. Avoid the issues in the beginning, with the understanding that a solution will be needed eventually.* *(YouTube did have to deal with pirated copyrighted content later, but since the company focused on user generated content, I'm treating this point as minimal for the Why Now analysis.)*	*Not a top driver of timing in 2005.*

2) Draw diagrams for the above list.

- If any of these stopped growing, which would have the biggest impact on YouTube?
- Draw trend lines based on industry market research (what already happened) and projections for the trend (dashed lines).
- Input your own perspective as well.

Driver: Technology
Moore's Law

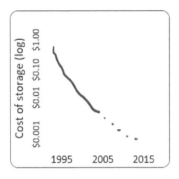

Driver: Technology
Edholm's Law

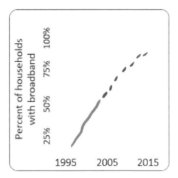

- Cost of data storage (to host video files) is declining rapidly
- If future videos are longer or higher quality, file size may increase, lessening the impact of falling prices

- Access to fast Internet in the home is at critical mass and increasing rapidly

Driver: Installed Base
Digital camera shipments

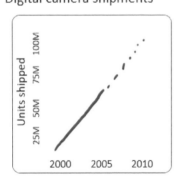

Driver: Social/Behavioral
Personal sharing: text & images

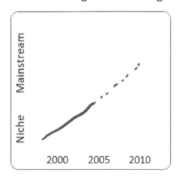

- Digital cameras are replacing film cameras
- Shipments are growing fast

- Sharing personal details becomes normal
- Expectations for continued activity
- Photo sharing sites become popular

3) Now let's look at why earlier attempts at streaming video partially succeeded or failed. What has changed since then?

    Earlier attempts at video streaming include:

- The band Severe Tire Damage played the first Internet concert in 1993. The concert was broadcast live at Xerox PARC with video and audio carried over the highspeed MBONE (IP Multicast Backbone) and using a significant amount of all Internet bandwidth available. The band then opened for The Rolling Stones in another online show in 1994. Sound and video quality was poor.
- Real Networks RealVideo Player (1997) could stream video and vary the number of frames per second depending on connection and computer processing power.
- Blockbuster / Enron Broadband Services (2000, not launched) focused on the distribution of existing copyrighted content. Required a TV and a device.
- Hong Kong Telecom iTV (1998 to 2002) required TV, a set top box, and high-speed Internet. Users experienced long delays when trying to load videos and little content to choose from.
- Shareyourworld.com (1998 - 2001) enabled users to upload and share their own videos. The company was without a revenue model and had bandwidth problems, but benefitted from cameras becoming cheaper.

4) Competitors. Now add the recent companies delivering similar services. (Remember that we're using an example from 2005.)

- PutFile launched early 2004. Provided video hosting, with ratings.
- Vimeo launched in late 2004. Some problems with the technology. Owned by CollegeHumor, which helped with distribution.

- Google Video launched early 2005. Targeted existing content, rather than user generated content.
- 24 Hour Laundry (24HL) launched in 2005. Focused on video hosting and blogging.
- Dailymotion launched in 2005.
- Other video companies focused on adult content and were unlikely to move to the mainstream market. I'm not counting them in the list.

5) Build the **Timing Map**. Make diagrams of the main drivers. For each chart I marked "too early" with a dotted vertical line.

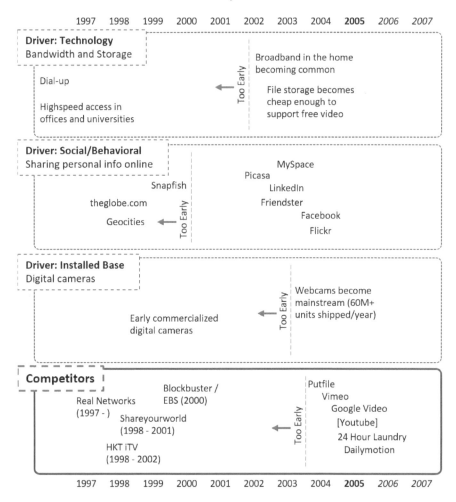

6) Map the results of the Why Now Session to your business model

Before the changes outlined above, a *non-streaming* video business worked like this:

Video content is mainly created by professionals on formats like videotapes, DVDs, or sometimes digital storage. Sharing videos can be a hassle: videocassettes are bulky, DVDs are smaller but still need to be physically mailed, and video files are too large for email. Even when you upload a video online, there are issues with file formats, limited compression, and the need for specific players. The primary way to make money with videos is by selling or renting physical copies.

Putting that legacy video business into the three-part business model format.

Legacy Video Companies

Value created for your customers	$>$	Value captured by the business	$\geq$	Cost to provide the value
• Professionally created videos • Can rent or purchase videotapes and DVDs on many topics • Video discoverability via catalogs		• Rental revenue from physical copies • Sale revenue from physical copies		• Production costs • Licensing fees • Cost of distribution via rental or sales outlets • Videotape and DVD costs

And before the changes outlined above, a *streaming* video business (for example, one that launched in the late 1990s) would have an out-of-balance business model like this:

Streaming Video Companies in the 1990s

Value created for your customers	?	Value captured by the business	$\leq$	Cost to provide the value

• Some ability to make and share user-generated videos, depending on device and broadband access • Some ability to watch other's videos, depending on device and broadband access	• Possible ad revenue	• High hosting costs • High bandwidth costs • High cost to build and maintain platform

But with the timing drivers that affected YouTube, all three elements of the business model radically changed.

Files were big but storage was cheap. Sharing video became easy. Posting videos online was common, file formats were few, and compression was powerful. It became possible to monetize through advertising and subscription offers.

Streaming Video Companies Around 2005

Value created for your customers	>	Value captured by the business	≥	Cost to provide the value
• Lots of user-generated video variety and ability to search and share • Commenting and community options • Recommended videos based on view history		• Potential ad revenue based on views and targeting • Eventually subscriptions		• Hosting costs • Bandwidth costs • Costs of platform building and maintenance

In your own work, you should be able to add numbers to the three parts of your business model. Or at least the second two parts. The first part (value created for your customers) can be harder to assess, especially for consumer products.

For business customers the first part of the business model can be more straightforward as business customers can tell you how much they value a product or how much its absence costs them. But for consumer products, even if there's no dollar figure, the value created for customers should be recognizably much higher than the value captured. Otherwise, why would they buy?

Going through this business model step enables your team to describe the business model impact of the future state of the business. Work toward that future state in your projections and presentations.

Without checking against the business model, the Why Now Session can leave you with an explanation for why something is now possible, but no explanation for how you can make a financially sustainable business out of it.

Returning to the introduction's first chart, we can see that video competitors from the 1990s (Shareyourworld, Hong Kong Telecom iTV, Blockbuster / Enron Broadband Services) were in the "dangerously early" phase. They all failed. That clump of video companies from around YouTube's time (Putfile, Google Video, 24 Hour Laundry, Vimeo, Dailymotion) were in the middle "market window opens" phase. Half of them failed (Putfile, Google Video, 24 Hour Laundry). Later specialty or niche video platforms that emerged after this case study (for example, Crunchyroll, Viddsee, Mobli, and Periscope) would be in the "not too late" phase.

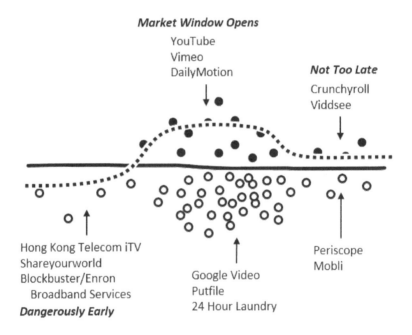

YouTube founders and management also made good decisions. Helping with distribution, YouTube transcoded different video file formats to compressed Flash video, the most common format at the time. Other video companies of YouTube's era made tactical errors, had poor management, or didn't improve their slow video load time. Those examples are important, but aren't included in a Why Now Session, except as additional context.

Depending on who you present to, you might not want to share all the details that came out of your Why Now Session. As a summary, put your findings in a readable single slide when you pitch for investment or present your company. The result of this exercise is that when you do speak about your business and its timing benefits, you can have a much deeper discussion about your perspective. If desirable, you can also share the extra content in a more detailed presentation.

Skip the above steps and you'll risk a superficial understanding of your timing advantage. By going through the above process you'll also have the content for a more detailed version that you might want to share with some audiences, such as your Challengers (which we'll introduce later).

Now that we've done YouTube's Why Now Session, what would a summary slide look like? Here's my version.

YouTube - Why Now

- Ongoing habit for people to share their lives online (text and image sharing are established, video is next).

- Broadband to the home is becoming mainstream (50% penetration and growing at double digits/year).

- Digital storage is cheap and getting cheaper (cost to store a video under $0.01, making advertising models possible).

- Growth in digital camera usage (more people can record and upload video easily).

These changes are converging to make this the time to build a video streaming business.

After the Why Now Session

Now that you've seen the YouTube case study, let's go deeper into next steps after the session.

Challenging the Session

Because it's likely that a serious audience will challenge parts of a Why Now presentation, go through this exercise yourself before you invest serious time building or before presenting to investors or those approving budgets.

Take the above points and run a Challenge Session. The purpose is to check the research and logic you're using, asking the question: "Why *Not* Now"?

To do that, put together an audience.

For those of you who are the audience, read up on the Why Now concept, timing drivers, and other supporting information in this book. Once you have the background, here's a template for you to challenge the Why Now Session.

Challenge	Agree/Disagree. Details.
1. Do the chosen drivers of timing make sense? Has there really been a change that is opening a window of opportunity?	
2. Are we too early? Are we far enough away from expected changes that the business will not be able to survive long enough to benefit? Or that the product team won't survive?	

3. Is the market window likely to remain open long enough for the business to take advantage of it? Or is this a fad – a small opening for a business that cannot move quickly?	
4. If there are combinations of drivers, do they strengthen the timing advantage?	
5. Do the future expectations seem forced or are they plausible? What supports the expectations?	
6. Who else could also take advantage of this timing situation? Who might we have to compete against?	
7. Are we forgetting something about what won't change that invalidates the Why Now? (Remember Jeff Bezos' quote from the beginning of the book: "What's not going to change in the next 10 years?")	
8. What current investment bias might skew our decision to move ahead? Does increased attention to a hot industry lead to decisions without serious thought? Do dismissals of other industries lead us to ignore opportunities?	
9. Is the new business model realistic? Do we have sufficient evidence?	
10. What else would invalidate the timing assessment?	

To have a deeper discussion on timing, go back a few steps. For the drivers you have listed, do you agree with the assessment of why they emerged? Can you explain the changes in some other way?

Do you agree with the selection of the top drivers? Do you agree with the projections listed?

For example, if you have Technology as a driver, what created the change on the technology side? Was it a result of Moore's Law, where all companies might benefit from lower costs and better performance? Or was the technology benefit driven by additional production? The related resources might be in high demand and rising in price (like GPU production for the gaming industry that then powered the crypto and AI industries).

If Regulatory/Legal is a driver, could it swing back in the other direction? If something else drove the change, is it likely to remain long-term (for example, telehealth being accepted by insurance companies at the start of COVID, but likely to remain even post-pandemic)?

You won't know the actual answers to these questions until the change has already happened and the Why Now question has drifted into the past. There is also no definite foresight since the answers unfold over time and can be changed by the actions of many other actors and their unexpected effects. But you'll have one or more positions on how you think things will go.

A note on the time allotted for the Challenge Session. Above I recommended one hour, with a little time at the beginning for presenting the Why Now.

That's not much time to go through the questions I list above.

To have a productive session, the challenge team should receive the Why Now Session information in advance – both the summary and the supporting Timing Maps. The challenge team should then read those before the Challenge Session. That way you'll have a productive meeting.

Rework After the Challenge

After receiving feedback in the Challenge Session, you may want to do more research and rework your presentation.

The most common types of rework I've seen to be valuable are:

- Rethinking the way earlier businesses failed. Did they fail because they didn't work well enough (like streaming video over dial-up Internet) or because there was no demand for the products? Or because of an unsustainable business model, bad management, or something else?

- Rethinking your assessment on the speed of change. Regarding your industry and relevant drivers, are you in a period of predictable change or chaotic change? Do you expect the situation to change slowly and predictably, quickly and predictably, or in some highly uncertain way? Any of these options could be fine, depending on what you're building.

- Catching incorrect dates, data, and weak assumptions.

Edit and go through the Challenge Session one more time if you need.

Avoid the Analysis of Others

In the Why Now Session I ask you to research existing and forecast demand for relevant products. However, this is different from looking at research that predicts demand for your own product.[7]

Here's what I mean. In your supporting research, you should look at what's changing in drivers that support your business arriving at the right time. Look for the converging factors that make this the right time for your product to exist. (Of course, you might find that there are no drivers in your case.)

But sometimes people are tempted to look at the timing question in an unhelpful way.

A tempting approach is to look up analyst reports of future demand for your industry or product, choose the big numbers, and use them to support your case.

Don't do that. Here's why.

Below is a series of analyst estimates from 2016 for the potential size the virtual reality and augmented reality market would reach in a few years. I chose 2016 since VR and AR received a lot of attention then. That was the year many people expected the technologies to break out.

Take a look at these quotes from analyst reports from back then.

- "[T]he market for VR products and technologies was valued at $1.37 billion in 2015 and is expected to reach $33.9 billion by 2022. The overall market for AR was valued at $2.35 billion in 2015 and is expected to reach $117.4 billion by 2022."[8]

- "According to the report, the global virtual reality (VR) market was valued at approximately USD 2.02 billion in 2016 and is expected to reach approximately USD 26.89 billion by 2022, growing at a CAGR of around 54.01% between 2017 and 2022."[9]

- "The virtual and augmented reality market will reach $162 billion by 2020."[10]

- "Forrester's report estimated the demand for virtual reality headsets in the U.S. will mean there'll be 52 million devices in the country by 2020."[11]

Now let's look at reports published in 2020 about the actual state of VR and AR in that year.

- "The global virtual reality software and hardware market size was valued at $2.6 billion in 2020, which will jump to $3.7 billion in 2021, $4.6 billion in 2022, and $5.1 billion by 2023 (SuperData, 2020). As of 2020, 26 million VR headsets are owned by consumers globally (CNBC, 2020). The combined augmented reality and virtual reality markets were worth $12 billion in 2020 with a massive annual growth rate of 54%, resulting in a projected valuation of $72.8 billion by 2024 (IDC, 2020)."[12]

- "The global virtual reality market is projected to grow from $6.30 billion in 2021 to $84.09 billion in 2028 at a CAGR of 44.8% in the forecast period, 2021-2028."[13]

- 5.5 million VR and AR devices were shipped globally in 2020.[14]

What wildly different outcomes in only four years. The expectations from 2016 were much higher than what reality served up in 2020. Ridiculously higher, even though the predictions and reality are only a few years apart.

Importantly, the above also says nothing about VR and AR business models. Is there theoretical high demand, but only at prices that are currently unsustainable?

My point isn't to pick on VR and AR market analysts. There have been many industries that seemed promising that later fell short of expectations in market size or speed of growth. If you're using other people's forecasts to justify your own timing, you're skipping the process and simply looking for big numbers that legitimize what you've already decided to do.

You are also missing the point of thinking about timing and running a Why Now Session. You need to approach the Why Now Session from the perspective of learning about drivers that are relevant to your business, not by simply choosing research that agrees with you.

Plus, if you just repeat analyst quotes, when you meet someone who doubts the numbers, the best response you can give is "that's what they say."

But why were the analyst reports wrong?

It's hard to know without seeing their process, but I suspect something other than methodology as the prime cause.

What gets reported and repeated are the big numbers, the big potential opportunities, the stories of how the world will change in the near future. Teams seeking investment and even investors seeking justification for their investments will be tempted to stress the optimistic outlooks. So will analysts. It's more noteworthy to publish research claiming a big change is on the way, rather than research saying that the world will remain the same.

Another risk is that in certain industries, analysts curry favor with the businesses they cover. That means that publishing a negative report harms their access and ability to charge for research reports.

If you're presenting your own Why Now, relying on analyst reports without understanding the underlying drivers opens you up to being challenged by someone who doesn't believe the reports. Instead, if you present your reasoning behind the way drivers will affect outcomes and the timing for that, you'll have a discussion.

But what about the way I ran through the YouTube analysis in the earlier section? I did use analyst reports on a number of projections, including on digital cameras and webcam sales, expected broadband penetration growth, and on the cost of digital storage. I also showed what people had already done, such as the number of cameras purchased and social media and online image sharing that was already taking place.

But there were a couple differences in my YouTube research and the VR / AR examples I showed above.

For some of the research I showed, the world had already reached the point where enough supporting drivers were in place. File storage was already cheap and was continuing to predictably decline in cost. Broadband penetration to the home was already common and people were not about to go back to dial-up. Digital cameras and webcams were already common and people were unlikely to go back to videocassettes.

The supporting drivers were already in place for user-generated video content (the product) and interest was already there.

That list is different from the VR / AR projections on how many units would ship – projections that people would start to do something different in the future. It's similar to the earlier Jeff Bezos quote on remembering what won't change.

If you're evaluating someone's Why Now and you question them using a set of analyst reports you trust, make sure you understand the drivers of the expected changes.

If you're evaluating someone's Why Now and you instead see a reliance on analyst reports, talk through their logic.

If someone pushes back on your Why Now with an analyst report that they trust, ask how the analyst came to their conclusions. Is the disagreement on how fast the change will happen or on its magnitude? Is there an appreciation for the way multiple drivers may converge?

Simply reporting that a changing industry will be a certain size in so many years doesn't give you much useful information. Having a rationale for why that industry could grow to a certain size in so many years does give you useful information.

Videophones

It became normal to communicate by video in the 2010s, but specific

---

devices called videophones had been around for decades by that time.

But videophones were financial failures for the companies that commercialized them. The biggest failure came from AT&T, which spent $500M (over $4 billion in adjusted 2024 dollars) developing their Picturephone service. The Picturephone was an early device enabling two callers to have a live audio and video conversation.

After demos at the 1964 World's Fair, AT&T brought the first version to market in 1970 and 1971. A three-minute call cost $16 (equal to $216 in 2024). Result? Few customers and calls.

In 1982 AT&T launched the Picturephone Meeting Service, for corporate video conferencing. Cost at the time: $1,340 for a 1-hour video call (equal to $4,440 in 2024). Another attempt in 1992, the Videophone 2500, had a color screen. AT&T tried to solve the critical mass issue by selling the equipment in pairs. That version cost $1,500 (later $1,000) or $30 for an overnight rental. It too failed.

For a new product launch, videophones like these also had a specific Installed Base problem that was different from what later cell phone product launches experienced.

Mobile phone users could call anyone with a phone number, whether another mobile phone or a landline. But to make a video call, videophone customers needed others with the same type of videophone.

Until the late 1990s, at least nine companies entered the videophone market before ultimately failing.

Video communications only took off when users no longer needed specialized video devices and could instead use laptops or smartphones with built-in cameras.

AT&T also had the prescience to believe that the days of voice-only communications would eventually come to an end. The Picturephone, needing extra bandwidth to relay moving images, would require a network upgrade. Legacy copper cable to the home would not be enough. Sales from the Picturephone would fund the eventual high speed network buildout. But it didn't happen back then.

Early Videophone Drivers - weak or non-existent: tech (bandwidth issues, limited processing power, high production costs), social/behavioral (uncertain need for video communications), installed base (lack of devices), networks (critical mass not yet achieved).

Later Video Communications Drivers - strong: tech (bandwidth is solved, cheap processing power), social/behavioral (expectation of video communications), installed base (devices are already distributed), networks (critical mass already achieved).

Some product leaders depend on off-the-shelf analyst reports or take a static view of the world. Even when they identify a trend, they give no thought to what drives the trend, even if it is something random or difficult to measure. If we only look at the existing snapshot and not the underlying drivers, then we don't develop a perspective on the direction things can go.

You probably don't have $500M (or $4B) to spend on that.

Don't Do This: Running a Bad Why Now Session

Just as we can fool ourselves into thinking that we're on the right track when we're not, we might also force a Why Now Session to portray a strong opportunity where none exists.

But that's a problem. We're either fooling others or fooling ourselves.

What does a bad Why Now Session look like? Here are some telltale signs. Don't do these things.

- Pushing the work off to someone not deeply engaged in decision making, product development, or funding.

- Avoiding research on the supporting drivers and previous failed attempts at building similar products.

- Relying on research showing future demand for the thing you are making, rather than understanding the underlying drivers of change.

- Relying on beautifully designed slides to distract from the lack of substance.

There are successful businesses that don't benefit from timing. Don't try to force the "good timing" story where none exists.

Don't Do This: Running a Bad Challenge Session

We want the Why Now Session to be challenged because that helps improve it.

If you're on a Challenge Team and don't try to pick apart the timing assessment, you'll leave that team with potential gaps in their work and less able to defend themselves when they actually pitch for funding or resources.

Why do we do this? It's uncomfortable to dissect someone's arguments. Then again, sometimes we like to criticize too much in the wrong way.

What does a bad Challenge Session look like?

- The team doesn't have the authority, confidence, or care, to stand up and challenge the assessment.

- The team didn't review the information in advance and then finds it difficult to comment on the findings in real time.

- The team is too distant from the information presented. Even after reviewing the Why Now Session findings they don't understand the meaning deeply enough.

- The team is too critical and rejects the Why Now Session findings too aggressively as an excuse to shut down an internally unpopular project.

- The team focuses on minor details rather than the big picture.

The Challenge Team is there to check whether the timing assessment is valid. Don't avoid this important responsibility.

The Cloud

In 1996 Oracle announced their development of the "Network Computer," a computer with no hard drive. The purpose was to cut the cost of storage space and build inexpensive terminals that would connect to the Internet to access data.

If you consider the network computer idea from the present you might

---

come to different conclusions than people did in 1996 when digital storage was much more expensive and Internet bandwidth much less available.

But a decade after the Network Computer launch, the above points flipped. Storage space had become cheap. High-speed internet access and Wi-Fi was normal.

Our dependence on the Cloud has grown in the past 25 years. I wrote this entire book in the cloud using Google Docs. In 1996 I would have used a local copy of Word.

As Oracle CEO Larry Elisson said at the 1995 International Data Corp European IT Forum: *"The mainframe is not dead; it is just not at the center of the universe. At the center of the universe is the network. A PC is a ridiculous device; the idea is so complicated and expensive. What the world really wants is to plug in to a wall to get electronic power and plug in to get data."*

But Oracle's launch may have originated in a desire to neutralize the growing popularity of Windows, rather than an actual business need or why now.

In terms of timing, other people involved in the network computer went on to bring the concept out in different ways. One was the former CTO of Sun Microsystems. Sun had developed the Java programming language, which was widely used in websites at the time. That CTO was Eric Schmidt, later CEO of Google.

Another proponent at the time was an SVP at Oracle. That was Marc Benioff, who founded Salesforce.com, a company based on cloud applications.

But Oracle's timing was off. Plus, in the rush to deliver the first Network Computers, they built crude versions that were slow to render web pages (something that the machine needed to do well).

Over four years, Oracle lost over $170 million on this business line.

But in the next decade, the time for network computer-like devices started to be right.

The term "Netbook" was popularized by ASUS, which launched its Eee PC line in 2007. Netbooks came without floppy drives, legacy ports for printer connections or external CD drives. They had limited storage space (solid state rather than spinning magnetic disks). Netbooks were also cheaper than other options.

But the biggest impact from the network computer model was in distributed computing power that was rented rather than owned.

Amazon Web Services (AWS) launched in 2006, just seven years after Oracle shut down its Network Computer project. By 2020, AWS had become a $46 billion business line for Amazon.

However, Amazon came to the cloud in a very different way than Oracle came to the Network Computer. While Oracle used the Network Computer as a foil to Microsoft, Amazon first built AWS for itself. While Oracle tried launching in an unsupportive infrastructure environment, Amazon did not face that challenge.

Amazon's concept was a bit different from the original Network Computers in that AWS enabled developers to build and deploy applications more quickly. Developers didn't need to spend time setting up their own infrastructure for data storage, security, uptime management, and maintenance and could instead use AWS.

Drivers: tech (Moore's Law / processing power and costs, Edholm's Law / bandwidth), networks (devices are networked), available talent (fewer team members needed to manage infrastructure),

Timing Drivers

As another way to introduce the timing drivers, I made a set of diagrams to provide ideas for how they work.

Use the examples below to think through your timing drivers.

Select from this list and add to it as it suits your situation.

Note that these are presented as general examples. With your industry knowledge, your timing driver examples can be much more specific.

Technology: Performance Curves

Technology drivers change what you can build. What was too slow, too expensive, or impossible becomes fast, cheap, and possible.

Some types of incremental tech progress is predictable on a rough timeline while other radical types are not. There are "laws" like Moore's Law and more that describe how fast we may see these changes.

For example, computing power went from exorbitant and rare to cheap and plentiful. All the computing power used in the Apollo moon mission was less than what's now easily available on a cheap smartphone.

We see such improvements in many technology-related endeavors.

The price of solar power, the yield of farmland, the size of devices needed for digital storage… the cost to sequence a human genome, to produce lab grown meat, to put a kilogram into orbit, … all these have improved over the years and often dramatically. With recent developments in generative AI, we expect that we'll see even more performance curve improvements.

This isn't just about modern examples. Performance curves go way back. It's just that the improvements took longer.

In 1800, buying an hour of nighttime light (at the average wage) with candles cost 5.4 hours of labor. By 1855 kerosene lamps offered one hour of light at 0.23 hours of work. By 1910 electric lights turned that ratio into one hour for 0.09 hours of work. And by 1960, 0.001 hours of work.[15]

Today, an hour of light is so cheap we rarely consider it.

Key questions: On what timeline will relevant technology improvements benefit our work?

Here are visualized examples from computing power and data communications.

Driver: Technology

Moore's Law

- The number of transistors on a microchip doubles every 18-24 months
- What was formerly too slow or expensive becomes fast and cheap

Edholm's Law

- Bandwidth and data speeds double every 18 months
- Fixed, nomadic (semi-portable wireless connectivity), and wireless communications converge in speed

Social/Behavioral: The Enduring Human Condition, Fads, and More

Social and Behavioral drivers can offer surprises.

There are enduring human needs that seem like they'll never go away, as long as there are people. A short list would include the need for housing and food as well as the enduring love of music and entertainment.

There are also new habits that emerge. Over the centuries, as people started drinking coffee and tea, those products came to be commercialized in more ways. People also started to drink alcohol in many forms, sometimes commonly in the evening and at other times and places in history, from breakfast until dinner. What determines what's normal?

We can see hints of what is to come by looking for niches of the new behavior. Will it spread? Or is the niche enough for our business?

Key questions: Where are the niches? Are they new or enduring behaviors? What's the half-life of new products?

Driver: Social/Behavioral

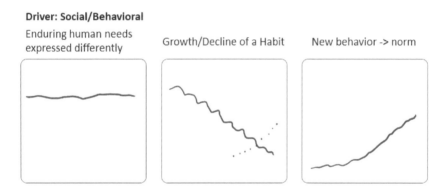

Enduring human needs expressed differently   Growth/Decline of a Habit   New behavior -> norm

Enduring Human Needs, Expressed Differently

- Universal love of music
- Need to feel important
- Need to provide for self and family

Growth or Decline of a Habit

- Smoking is dangerous: cigarette smoking declines in the US for years. Eventually, vaping replaces cigarettes. Vaping is better, but still dangerous…
- Fat is bad: fat-free, sugary foods become popular. Sugar is bad…

Strange New Behavior Becomes the Norm

- Internet use goes from atypical to common
- Online dating goes from fringe to mainstream

Regulatory/Legal: Prohibitions and Requirements

Regulatory and legal drivers describe the way products are prohibited or required because of governmental and legislated decisions. Some types of businesses and products face close control, only to be allowed later on. Sometimes those prohibitions or requirements operate cleanly – like an on/off switch. And sometimes there's a lot of flexibility. In those cases, regulatory/legal drivers are more like a dimmer switch.

For example, the cannabis industry, which operated in a gray or black market for much of the last century, has been coming into the mainstream in the US as a result of changed regulations. New financial instruments like cryptocurrencies can go from unknown, to encouraged, to outlawed. Popular businesses can also influence regulations and laws, for example as Airbnb did to continue operating even though it should have required a hotel license in many markets. Many telecom innovations, like Internet Telephony and complicated routing paths, came from avoiding regulatory restrictions.

In some cases, there is predictability to these changes. For example, when something is patented, the patent holder has a set number of years to commercialize the invention while having some ability to prevent others from copying them. Some industries, like 3D printing and ecommerce, grow when key patents expire.

Less predictable changes include new legislation that is influenced by public interest groups or lobbyists, changing public opinion, and elections that affect who votes on rules.

Key questions: Do we have any impact on regulations and laws? When do the regulations and laws come into force? What's the industry response?

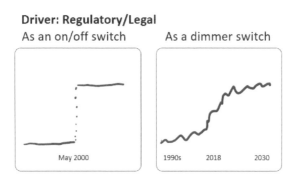

Driver: Regulatory/Legal

As an on/off switch   As a dimmer switch

47

On/Off Switch

- Accurate GPS (managed by US government) allowed for civilians starting May 2000
- Many 3D printing patents expired in the 2010s

Dimmer Switch

- Cannabis legal locations and situations increase

Installed Base: Existing Devices or Systems

Installed Base drivers rely on the existence of another product that the new business will ride on top of.

For example, while the components that supported rideshare (GPS, handheld communications tech, online payments, rating systems) were already established, it took years until smartphone penetration, device capabilities, and the app stores combined them all. Building Lyft and Uber before then would have been technically possible, but much more difficult. The earlier installed base of Garmin and TomTom GPS devices did not enable ridesharing, because those devices were only used by drivers, not passengers, and couldn't handle payments or ratings, among other limitations.

Devices in use may enable something new. And your business can ride on top of that installed base rather than developing it yourself.

In some situations, it's essential that there be an installed base before a new entrant could possibly succeed.

Imagine if Snapchat and Instagram also had to make smartphones and create the app stores. It would be too complex and expensive for those products to exist.

Key questions: What installed base can we leverage to shorten our time to market? Are we at risk of overreliance on an installed base?

Driver: Installed Base

Devices in use   Features of devices

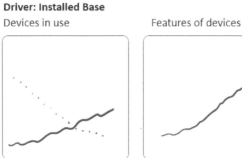

Devices in Use

- Feature phones (those with press-button inputs and no touch-sensitive display) replaced by smartphones
- Nokia and Blackberry centrally managed apps (where app developers had to sell the handset maker on their apps) replaced by Apple iOS and Android app stores (where end users decided on the apps they wanted to use)

Features of Devices

- Digital cameras are common and built into laptops
- Front-facing cameras in smartphones

Crisis: The Wildcard

Whatever the situation, a **Crisis** can change things quickly. Crises can change the speed and direction of processes and result in unexpected outcomes.

Examples include the sudden increase in remote work, deliveries, ecommerce, telemedicine, and more during COVID.

What was assumed to be the status quo unexpectedly changes quickly, causing the crisis. Note that the speed of change is what creates the crisis. It's not only that the change is judged to be bad.

There is a crisis somewhere in the world every single day. Crises can also be invented or exaggerated for specific purposes.

Key questions: Can we move fast enough to take advantage of the crisis?

Driver: Crisis

Accelerations   New reality   Wildcard

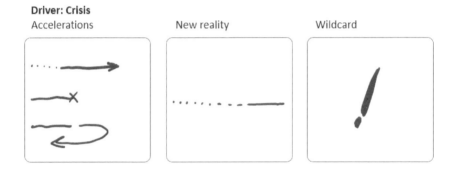

Accelerations

- Speeds up a process
- Slows down or blocks a process
- Reverses a process

New Reality

- Starts as a temporary fix and becomes permanent

Wildcard

- Crises enable the introduction of something new and formerly unlikely

51

Economic: Ups and Downs

Economic drivers reflect changes in the economy you operate in.

We consider this as a driver because economic drivers affect your viability, customer needs, and customer behavior.

We often act as though change in the economy is slow and predictable. But unpredicted and poorly explained economic turmoil happens frequently. In spite of that, people often act like shocks are uncommon.

If the economy is a timing driver, what drives the driver itself? Many things, including innovation, government-set interest rates, war, demand shifts, demographics, and many of the other drivers mentioned here. It's influenced by the trust that people have in their government and the connected decisions others make around the world.

I'm not suggesting that you should try to predict economic growth and then use that to guide your timing analysis. Well, maybe beyond a short-term horizon. The economic driver can benefit those who can act quickly when there's an unexpected change, which happens quite a bit.

Key questions: What impact does economic growth or decline have on our product? Do we trust growth expectations?

Driver: Economic

Projected growth   Economic shock

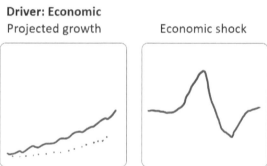

Projected Growth

- Growth projections in different markets

Economic Shock

- Sudden increased income -> Make risky investments
- Sudden lost income -> Rent out assets (homes)

Networks: Connections and Flows

Different from Installed Base, **Network** drivers create opportunities through their connections.

Network drivers are affected by the number of nodes (for example devices or people), connections between them, and how communication flows between nodes.

The existence of a network connects people. Access to such a network, by being a member, a customer, a contributor, can open up new opportunities.

The network may also rely on different supporting infrastructure. For example, the existence of online social networks enabled new forms of content distribution, selling, and subscription models. The connections were the key, rather than the equipment people used. Traditional networks enabled trust at a distance and new forms of commerce.

Key questions: How do networks impact us? If our product is not network relevant today, should we make it so? What kind of network do we have or could we build?

Driver: Networks

As an enabler   Metcalf's Law

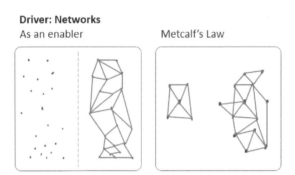

Networks as an Enabler:

- Telecom network
- Alumni network
- Neighborhood or social network

Metcalfe's Law

- The value of a network rises with the number of its connections (is proportional to the square of the number of network nodes). More nodes, more value

Distribution: Reaching Your Customers and Resources

New types of **Distribution** moves physical things and digital information from one place to another better, faster, cheaper.

New forms of distribution enable some types of business. For example, development of the printing press in Europe led to mass produced pamphlets and cheaper books that helped spread the ideas that led to the Protestant Reformation (earlier religious movements failed or were limited). Online communities form a new kind of distribution opportunity to tap into. Distribution may come from a combination of other drivers, but functions as its own driver.

These changes in distribution can be discontinuous, for example when a new method is developed and popularized.

Key questions: What impact does distribution have on the success of our product? Who controls our distribution?

Driver: Distribution

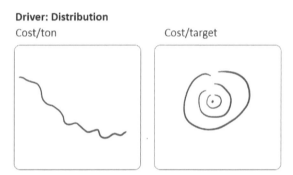

Cost/ton   Cost/target

Cost per Item

- Third-party logistics, local delivery, international freight services, shipping containers

Cost per Target

- Online targeting, niche campaigns become possible
- Using new forms of distribution, either out of creativity or necessity (mainstream is off-limits or too expensive)

Capital Access: Funding, Investment Appetite, and Options

Capital Access changes over time with the economy, interest rates, evidence of success stories, and other trends.

Capital access varies at different times and locations. Who is the likely source of capital -- government, venture investors, traditional lenders, customers, or communities? What impact do low or high interest rates have on willingness to invest?

Key questions: Do we have an advantage in the current funding environment? What opportunities open or close because of capital access?

Driver: Capital Access

Venture Investing   Hot/cold industries   Alternative Capital

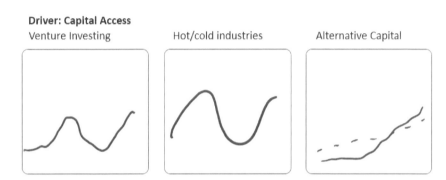

Venture Investing

- Investments over time
- Round sizes
- Geographic access

Hot or Cold Industries

- Previous experience with a specific industry (good or bad) creates or kills opportunities

Alternative Capital Sources

- Crowdfunding
- Loan programs
- Grant programs

Organizational: Risk, Efficiency, and Learning

Organizational drivers can be varied. They are about the way people organize themselves and resources. Innovations in these drivers affect what can be built and how.

Some of these organizational drivers are about the way we legally manage complex resources, some are about the way we build capabilities, and some are about the way organizations learn.

New organizational structures, including corporations (so individuals may be shielded from the risk the organization takes) and decentralized autonomous organizations (DAOs) for trustless accountability. Organizations learn as they gain and retain experience. Businesses may be able to produce more cheaply or without fixed costs by operating at scale or outsourcing production.

Key questions: Does our organization operate more effectively than others? How do available organization types impact the success of our product?

Driver: Organizational

Managing risk

Efficiency organizations

Wright's Law

Managing Risk

- Corporations
- Venture investing
- DAOs (digital autonomous organizations)

Efficiency Organizations

- Assembly line developed to organize unskilled labor
- School system designed to provide trained industrial workers

Wright's Law

- Every doubling in production results in a 20% cost reduction (experience curve)

Available Talent: The Builders

What **Available Talent** is there to support the building of specific products? What will these people need as they take new roles?

How are new talent pools trained? Where are they trained? Is training controlled by few designated organizations or can the market respond to additional demand? How fast can they be produced when demand increases?

Key questions: How can we benefit from talent production? How can we control access to talent so they seek opportunities with us rather than others?

Driver: Available Talent

University Grads by Degree   Globalization   Access Anywhere

University Graduates By Degree

- Rise or fall of specific majors
- Graduates in specific fields

Globalization

- Employment visas enabled temporary immigration and naturalization for some workers

Access Anywhere

- International or immigrant labor market
- Remote work

Demographic: Predictable and Projected

Demographic Drivers describe the way populations change over time. Some changes are predictable in advance (you need 25 years to grow a new group of 25-year-olds). And some change over time.

Population shifts are usually slow, studied, and predictable. The exception to that is smaller sudden shifts from immigration, war, refugees, and pandemics. What population segments experience at different times affects them long-term.

Key questions: How does our project respond to demographic change? Are we operating on a timeline where demographics are relevant?

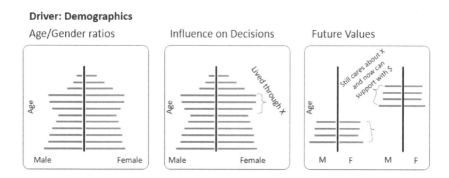

Driver: Demographics

Age/Gender Ratios

- The balance and weight of age/gender on the whole population

Influence on Decisions

- Perspectives formed by experience across time

Future Values

- Estimating what values in youth carry over as the demographic segment ages, shifts in the Overton window (the range of politically acceptable policies)

These are general examples. Your experience may not be described above. But you can use the categories to explore which drivers impact your business and what specifics you see in each.

Let's go on to other ways of looking at why now.

The Problem with Solving Problems

In new product development we're often told to look for problems and solve them. But this can produce reactive behavior. The problem must exist and be noticeable for there to be an opportunity to build a solution.

You might take a different approach for your own timing work.

As Alan Kay said in a 2014 Demo Conference talk titled The Future Doesn't Have to Be Incremental: *"We are a culture that is set up to do problem solving... [But] the essential process is "Problem Finding."*[16]

Once there's a problem and it's observable, it's true that you can start to build solutions. But solutions can be incremental improvements – where there's already a developed market with existing customers. As Kay also said in his talk: "Anything that is an obvious problem is some manifestation of the current worldview." And yet, some of the biggest markets today did not exist a short time ago.

My favorite example of this was the mid-1980s research that projected cellphone demand by the year 2000, conducted by McKinsey Consulting for AT&T. Result: the mobile phone market is too small. I've actually spoken to someone who was there in the room when the decision was made, following a presentation that showed the US cellular market capping out at 0.5% market penetration by the year 2000 (less than 1 million subscribers). They were off by a factor of over 100. AT&T sold off its mobile networks only to buy them back less than 10 years later for billions.

But I've also found that we can ask the problem question in ways that make just about anything seem like a problem to solve. When stressing the importance of solving problems we can project them backwards, even if business founders didn't originally take that approach.

For example, let's take rideshare businesses like Uber and Lyft that popped up around 2010. Today we might reevaluate Uber as solving the local transportation problem, but did people have a problem with local transportation back in 2010? They had buses, trains, cars, taxis, bikes, and could walk. Transportation was long since solved.

But those rideshare company founders had noticed timing drivers and then built for what was now possible, rather than an existing problem. By 2010 a critical mass of people carried GPS-enabled smartphones and it had become possible to locate passengers and navigate them to their destination (drivers: tech, installed base, networks).

Building those rideshare businesses might have been possible on smartphones a couple years earlier (say 2008 but with much worse real time navigation capabilities), or earlier on a different handheld device (maybe 2004, but much harder without an installed base of smartphones), or earlier than that had civilian access to accurate GPS been allowed pre-2000. But by 2010 all those timing drivers came together to open up the rideshare opportunity.

And the opportunity existed without the problem (transportation was already solved by taxis, trains, buses, rental cars, walking…) and with an existing market that was considered stable. That state of transportation was "just the way the world was."

Rather than only think about solving existing problems, think about taking advantage of new opportunities. Think about opportunities that could exist in the future.

Kay makes the following point about the tools you use to get to that future state: "Go into a university…go into most companies… they're computing on the computers of the past, and so the chance that they're going to do something that's non-incremental is almost zero. If you want to compute in the future, you have to compute with the computing power of the future because it actually is part of the thing that opens up the kinds of ideas that you can have."[17]

Where did Alan Kay practice "living in the future"? As part of Xerox PARC, which developed the Alto (an early personal computer), object-oriented programming, the laser printer, GUI (the graphical user interface that made it easy for people to interact with a computer), and desktop publishing, years before Apple. Inventions, that by his estimate, eventually produced $30 trillion in value.

A small team of 25 people at PARC developed those inventions. But as inventions, those early products didn't yet have sustainable business models. They were not innovations.

Here's a generalized image of the invention to innovation progression.

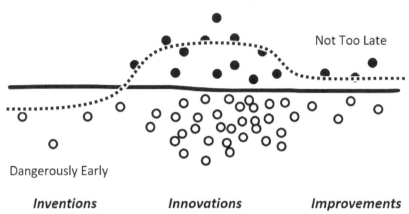

Inventions   **Innovations**   **Improvements**

Those early entrants developed new products, but released them without a supporting business model or many customers. An invention.

Later entrants observed those earlier products or learned from the past and concluded that there was potential for a sustainable business model currently or in an acceptable time. An innovation.

And even later entrants took existing products and business models, modified them, and possibly offered them to a niche. An improvement.

As Xerox didn't move to commercialize many of its inventions, some years later other companies, most famously Apple, did commercialize what had by then become business model-supported innovations. Jobs and others learned about those inventions because of his visit to PARC.

Who should get credit for making those inventions into business model-supported innovations? In 1983, Steve Jobs accused Bill Gates of stealing the concept for Microsoft Windows from Apple. But Gates' retort explained it all. Gates said: "Well, Steve… I think it's more like we both had this rich neighbor named Xerox and I broke into his house to steal the TV set and found out that you had already stolen it."[18]

The Alto computer, for example, adjusted for inflation to the year 2024, cost over $110,000. PARC was happy to pay that back in 1973 to get the computing power that would be normal in the late 1980s. It's surprising for many people to realize that it was possible to develop a personal computer in the early 1970s as long as it didn't need a sustainable business model.

Xerox killed the Alto project in 1977.

Iridium vs Cellphones

Iridium was one of the hottest and best funded startups of the 1990s, with support from its parent company Motorola, the originators of the first handheld mobile phones.

Conceived in 1987 and built from 1993 to 1998, Iridium's concept was revolutionary at the time. The company rolled out a network of satellites to enable phone calls from anywhere in the world.

But Iridium filed for bankruptcy in 1999, less than one year after service launch.

To evaluate their business timing, we have to remember that communications capabilities were different back then. Wireless connectivity was much more limited than today. Dead zones with no signal were normal. And when traveling internationally, mobile phones were sometimes useless because different countries used different mobile network technology and charged for international roaming.

After years of development and hype, Iridium launched in 1998 with a call between Vice President Al Gore and a great-grandson of Alexander Graham Bell. It took $5 billion to get to service launch.

But the world had changed. When Motorola started to work on Iridium there were only around 1 million mobile phone subscribers in the US. But at the time of launch in 1998, there were already 69 million US-based mobile subscribers and 300 million subscribers around the world.

Past mobile phone deployments depended on constructing cell towers, signing up subscribers, and linking communications services across networks. That required investing in expensive fixed assets needed to build mobile networks.

But by the time of Iridium's launch its why now had disappeared due to improvements of the previous 11 years of feature phone and mobile network development.

Iridium's phones were brick-sized and weighed about a pound. That size and weight may have worked in the late 1980s but by the late 1990s mobile phones had already become small and light.

Also notably, while people typically needed to make mobile calls while out and about in their cities, or from their offices or homes, few people needed to make a phone call from "anywhere," like a remote rural area or the middle of the ocean.

But Iridium's business model, with expensive satellites and quarterly payments to Motorola, required mass market adoption. The company didn't gain anything close to that.

Late 1990s mobile phones also became noticeably better multiple times a year. While Iridium's handset cost $3,000 in 1998 (equal to $5,800 in 2024) and calls were a few dollars a minute, feature phone handsets often cost only a few hundred dollars, with dramatically cheaper calls. Mobile networks grew and so did coverage.

Had communications tech not changed all that much during Iridium's 11 years of development and if there were no prospects for cheaper handsets, Iridium may have had a chance at survival. As it was, the company missed their time.

Iridium still exists though. Company assets were purchased in bankruptcy and Iridium now serves the extreme market of people working on remote infrastructure projects and soldiers in isolated areas.

Mistaking Capability for Desirability

We might have a perspective on timing drivers that will enable new businesses to emerge, but that doesn't mean that these businesses are inevitable.

As startup advisor Adam Berk puts it: "If you validate desirability but not capability, time can be on your side. If you validate capability but not desirability, time doesn't necessarily move the market your way."

That is, just because something becomes possible doesn't mean that people will want it.

Examples include: 3D TV, Google Glass as a consumer device, and the Segway.

What are some clues that if we do solve capability the desirability will follow? When does supply create demand? Where might inevitability come from?

Here are some ways to think about this question.

- For existing markets, is there desirability among a market segment that feels the pain the worst?

- For non-existing markets, are there potential customer personas who have a great need for something like the solution? Are there potential customer personas whose lives would be dramatically better with the solution?

- Is there desirability among those where money is not an object? Are people solving this problem today at high expense? Would others do so if not for the high price that is necessary because supply hasn't been solved?

- Is there something innate to the human condition about the desirability?

Mistaking Lack of the Product for the Lack of the Person

Alan Kay's perspective on finding problems gets at why we often have situations where there is unserved, hidden, latent demand that no customer directly expresses.

To me, it's the latent, tacit belief that "that's just the way the world is."

That belief keeps people from:

- Recognizing an opportunity.

- Believing it is possible to build something new.

- Attempting to build something new.

- Believing that what they build will succeed.

- Believing that people actually want the new thing.

As Kay also said in his talk, the part of the past that we recognize and use is small and distorted. Instead of being limited by what we accept as the past, we should open ourselves up to potential futures.

If there's latent demand for a solution but we don't see it being satisfied with a product, there might be something else going on. We might just be lacking the founder or team needed to make the thing.

What shortens the time to good timing? Founders with a curiosity or drive to build for the opportunity, supported intellectually, socially, and financially.

Those founders come from a broad range of places. They are industry outsiders as well as industry insiders. They are experienced as well as inexperienced.

What lengthens the time to good timing? A lack of founders dedicated to attacking an opportunity.

Those founders can be held back by negative drivers such as:

- A regulatory or legal environment that blocks development.

- Social or behavioral norms that make development unpalatable or unfashionable.

- A lack of capital access to build.

- A crisis that distracts founders from building.

- A belief that people like them or from places like theirs don't build these solutions.

- A lack of knowledge of what to do.

- A lack of role models to look to and exchange ideas with.

- Potential founders saddled with debt, family or other obligations, and unable to take needed risks.

Mistaking Lack of the Business for the Lack of the Capability

If desirability is present, something else can happen. We can mistake a lack of businesses taking advantage of new timing benefits for a lack of the capability itself.

Drawing the timing maps for those companies would show a "too early" line years before companies entered the market.

There are multiple reasons we don't see everything as soon as it becomes possible. There are:

- Unwillingness to invest in products without sustainable business models.

- Unpopular or toxic industries.

- Hype centered on other industries.

- People with relevant knowledge involved elsewhere.

- A bigger timing driver taking new business creation elsewhere.

- Drivers that counteract each other.

Timing Considerations

How should an organization choose to respond to timing opportunities?

The response should be different depending on organization capabilities and goals. But some things to consider include how fast the organization can move in response to the timing advantage noticed, whether it should be a first-mover or fast follower, likely time to pay back the initial investment, what others are likely to do, and more.

Here are some considerations as you navigate your way.

Competitive Effects

One of the best comments on the power of competition on outcomes is from Warren Buffet's 1985 Berkshire Hathaway shareholder letter:

"Over the years, we had the option of making large capital expenditures in the textile operation that would have allowed us to somewhat reduce variable costs. Each proposal to do so looked like an immediate winner…. But the promised benefits from these textile investments were illusory. Many of our competitors, both domestic and foreign, were stepping up to the same kind of expenditures and, once enough companies did so, their reduced costs became the baseline for reduced prices industrywide. Viewed individually, each company's capital investment decision appeared cost-effective and rational; viewed collectively, the decisions neutralized each other and were irrational (just as happens when each person watching a parade decides he can see a little better if he stands on tiptoes). After each round of investment, all the players had more money in the game and returns remained anemic."[19]

In this book I've said little about competition.

And yet, one of the major ways that beneficial timing can still fail comes down to getting outcompeted.

I've mostly left the competition topic aside, as the above quote from the textile industry is applicable to other industries, and the work others have done on competition is applicable to the timing situation.

But related to timing, we have the common "first mover" belief.

About First-Mover Advantage

You've probably heard the term "first-mover advantage," describing a claimed advantage enjoyed by the first entrant to a new market. During the Dotcom bubble, companies that brought existing products online used this concept as a rationale when they pitched for funding.

The "first-mover" term came from a paper written by Marvin Lieberman and David Montgomery, where the authors described the way entrants benefit or suffer depending on when they enter a market.

The common interpretation of first-mover advantage, popularized during the Dotcom-era, was that as an early entrant, the first mover would be more likely to win in a new market.

The problem was the paper's authors did not make that claim.

Lieberman and Montgomery offered a more nuanced view. They stated that while being a first-mover does offer some potential advantages, such as establishing brand recognition and customer loyalty, it also carries risks. These risks include the high market development costs, technological uncertainty, and the possibility of being overtaken by later entrants who learn from the first-mover's mistakes.

Studies of early market entrants show that first-movers are often not the ones that survive to win. In the study "Pioneer advantage: Marketing logic or marketing legend?" the researchers found that market pioneers failed more often than later entrants.[20] These later entrants, or "fast followers," aren't the first to offer a new product but succeed by improving upon the first-mover's offerings or benefitting from insights gained by observing the first-mover's journey. There are many examples of later entrants overtaking the pioneers by avoiding their early mistakes, leveraging more mature technologies, or better understanding customer needs.

In the case of the Dotcom bubble, many companies that were first to market with online versions of traditional services failed to sustain their lead. They struggled to scale their businesses or even just to build sustainable business models, a requirement of good timing. A common example is the way the online search industry changed, moving from early entrants like Alta Vista, Ask Jeeves, and Lycos on to a relatively late entrant, Google.

Creating a new market takes time. You have to educate your customers that they have the problem that your product solves. And in some cases, those future customers may not even believe that they have a problem.

But there are certainly successful first-movers that maintain their lead for years. The list includes FedEx, Intel, Southwest Airlines, eBay, and more.

And there are potential sources of first-mover advantage. If the first movers can control access to needed resources and develop organizational capabilities that are costly or difficult to duplicate, they may be able to delay or prevent the success of later entrants. If the first mover can gain significant market share before later entrants, then they can learn faster and maintain their success.[21]

Another way to think about maintaining an enduring lead is that rather than being first, companies should aim to be the one setting the "dominant design." In the beginning of a new product category, we tend to see many design types as companies explore potential ways to build products and serve new customers.[22]

But after a while, these designs converge into a dominant design that customers become comfortable with. Examples include everything from the Qwerty keyboard layout, to the enclosed automobile steel body, to the touchscreen smartphone with no keyboard.

In 1998 – the middle of the Dotcom bubble – the first-mover paper's authors wrote an update called "First-Mover (Dis)advantages."

To no avail.

First-mover advantage was used as a rationale for Dotcom-era startups to raise money for their too-early visions (and investors backing them). But those companies often had no supporting business model. They may have been first movers but they were not sustainable businesses.

Matching What Won't Change With What Is Changing

To repeat the earlier quote from Amazon founder Jeff Bezos:

"I very frequently get the question: 'What's going to change in the next 10 years?' And that is a very interesting question; it's a very common one. I almost never get the question: 'What's not going to change in the next 10 years?'"

What doesn't change serves as a baseline for your timing research. If you expect consistent demand for specific products (people will still eat, listen to music, and fall in love in the future) then you can apply that consistency as a baseline to what you notice is changing.

Old ways of living, behaving, and consuming are hard to abandon. It's often easier to replace something not with nothing, but with something new that can take its place.

Smoking, Anti-Smoking, and Vaping

Back in 2003, smoking laws changed in New York City. These changes doubled the price of a pack of cigarettes and eliminated indoor smoking sections in restaurants and bars.

The price increase reduced the number of cigarettes smoked.

But that price increase did something else too. It broke down the social bond shared by smokers.

Before the smoking ban it was common to hear: "Hey, could I bum a smoke from you?" After all, the cost of a single cigarette within a pack was only around $0.15 retail at the time, a price too low to care about.

After the ban, what you started to hear was: "Hey, do you have an extra cigarette? I have fifty cents." (A cigarette in the then average $7 pack of 20 cost the buyer $0.35.)

Another change from the smoking ban impacted smokers and non-smokers alike. The lack of the smell of smoke. Years ago, if you went out in many parts of the US (or most parts of the world) to a party or bar, it was common to be in a cloud of smoke. If you stayed long, your clothes stunk of smoke by the time you returned home. That was just the way it was.

Interestingly, the modern vaping products — the ones that became popular, unlike earlier attempts — were developed immediately after the New York City smoking ban.

Major tobacco companies including RJ Reynolds, BAT, and Philip Morris all had e-cigarette development programs and products decades before vaping became standard.

Those early smokeless cigarette products failed partly because of technology. It proved difficult to produce a nearly smokeless cigarette that also had qualities like low tar. The cigarettes often tasted terrible, required more effort to puff, and more importantly, looked ridiculous.

It wasn't until 2003 that pharmacist Hon Lik produced a better design

---

and vaping was born.

It took the anti-smoking focus on health and the regulatory ban to open a door for e-cigarette products.

It was also essential that vaping could claim to be less harmful than traditional cigarettes, but didn't require a total behavior change like nicotine patches and nicotine gum. Some groups not affiliated with tobacco companies ended up encouraging smokers to switch to vaping for health reasons. Smokers no longer needed to quit, they just needed to smoke differently.

Investors and Why Now

In the paper "How Do Venture Capitalists Make Decisions?," the authors surveyed over 800 VCs at over 600 firms to ask about their top considerations for making investments.[23]

More than 60% of responding VCs considered timing an important factor that contributed to successful investments (differences in rate depending on company stage) and approximately 10% considered timing to be the most important factor. For failed investments, timing was also listed as an important factor by more than 40% of VCs, with roughly 10% of VCs naming timing as the most important reason for the failure.

Then there's this comment from Charlie Munger, of Berkshire Hathaway on "surfing waves."[24]

"When new businesses come in there are huge advantages for the early birds. And when you're an early bird, there's a model that I call 'surfing.' When a surfer gets up and catches the wave and just stays there, he can go a long, long time. But if he gets off the wave he becomes mired in shallows. People get long runs when they're right on the edge of the wave— whether it's Microsoft or Intel or all kinds of people, including National Cash Register in the early days."

So you don't think that Munger's quote is just about being the first mover, remember that he referenced a "wave." That means that there already are forces (most likely outside of your control) that have converged. You notice that (and confirm it through a Why Now Session) and then enter. You are early compared to the others that haven't noticed the new opportunity. You have time to learn, build, and choose when to enter. Note also that many times, incumbents are often too entrenched in their way of doing things to surf their industry's next wave.

We don't always know it, but investors use timing in their own investment decisions. Roelof Botha, an investor at Sequoia, wrote about timing in his private YouTube investment memo from 2005, which was later made public.

Botha's memo outlined the progression of user generated content from shared text to images and argued that the next generation of content should turn out to be video, based on the spread of personal video cameras and broadband internet.

Botha wrote: "Digital video recording tech is for the first time cheap enough to mass produce and integrate into existing consumer products, such as digital photo cameras and cell phones, giving anyone the ability to create video content anytime, anywhere. As a result, user-generated video content will explode."

In his memo Botha also outlined the problem that existed in 2005: video content was difficult to share. Files were too large to email, too large to host, there was no standardization of file formats, and videos existed as isolated files without interaction between viewers or interrelation between videos.

Users uploaded videos and YouTube served the content to viewers. YouTube converted different video formats to Flash Video (Flash penetration was 97.6% of web users at the time). The videos were highly compressed and could stream instantly. Users didn't need to download the whole video first. Creating a community meant that people could comment on the videos and therefore would watch more.[25]

And back in 2005 broadband Internet into the home was also at critical mass. Traditional media also wanted to increase their online presence in order to follow their audience, which led to more interest in video. The timing was right for something like YouTube.

As much as I'm making a case for the importance of timing, my informal survey of investors and what I've seen myself reveals that most startups don't actually think deeply about timing and most pitches don't address the timing question.

As I've asked investors what they actually see when startups pitch, I've heard that only around 20% of startups are clear on what their timing advantage is. In a formal pitch, most don't actively present the role timing plays in their potential success. Those remaining 80% of startups are leaving it up to investors to apply their own perspective.

Another investor view of the timing question comes from Bill Gross, founder of early startup studio Idealab. Gross gave a short TED talk where he outlined his study of factors leading to startup success.[26]

Gross ranked 200 companies (both Idealab and others) on five factors: idea, team, business model, funding, and timing. He then estimated that 42% of company success was due to timing. He didn't share his data or process, but it's an interesting reference point. Contrasting his model and mine, I associate four out of five of his categories (all but idea) as being impacted by timing.

To compare, I looked into companies I've worked with to see if timing held up as a factor in their success or failure. It did.

In my own research into startups I know well, I've seen similar effects. My largest single portfolio was the group of companies I worked with in the University of Southern California Incubator. These consist of a broad range of company types, varying levels of founder experience, and different economic climates (the years 2015 to 2021 in the sample). I didn't include the more recent years because those companies haven't had enough time to fail or succeed.

Of the 168 companies from that portfolio that have existed for at least two and a half years (range two and a half to nine years), the failure rate was 51% for those with a timing advantage but 70% for those without a timing advantage. It was even more extreme in the acquisitions. Eight out of the nine acquired had timing advantages.

	No Timing Advantage	Timing Advantage
Failed	70% (65)	51% (38)
Has Not Failed	30% (28)	49% (37)

Averages for the full portfolio.

Failed: 61%, did not fail: 39%. No timing advantage: 55%, has timing advantage: 45%.

Not every situation calls for you to assess timing advantages. But where you need to convince investors that you're on the right path, you can gain a lot by thinking through the way the world is changing and how you can benefit from it. How you can surf those waves that Munger and Napoleon mentioned.

Why Now Slides In Pitch Decks

There is a difference between stories presented in a pitch deck and real experience. But when it comes to timing questions, pitch decks are one common place you see them answered.

For example, VC firms Sequoia and Kleiner Perkins have a recommended slide order for startup founders pitching to them (shown below, with minor adjustments). Likewise, DocSend (a company that enables founders to track who reads their pitch decks) has published a similar observed slide order. In each case, a Why Now slide features in the first half of the pitch deck.

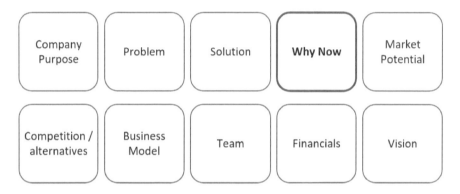

From DocSend's record of time spent per page, the Why Now slide ranked fourth (after financials, team, and competition).[27] That's either a mark of importance or a mark that Why Now slides were more interesting, controversial, or took more time to understand.

As part of my research I reviewed hundreds of Why Now slides in fundraising pitch decks. These slides tell the story that the team wants to promote, which means they often (but not always) show the most favorable parts of a timing advantage. But there is still something to learn from them.

Over hundreds of examples, I found patterns that I wrote up when I became fascinated by the timing topic.[28] A slide deck doesn't necessarily tell you what people truly think, but it does give you a clue as to what they think helps their situation.

From the slides I reviewed, both publicly available and private ones, I found a few styles.

There are helpful approaches:

- Identifying relevant timing drivers. Showing the combination of relevant timing drivers (even if they don't use that language) and how those drivers enable something new and powerful.
- Educating the audience. Helping investors or other reviewers to understand why the timing is right when they might not have the relevant background.
- Explaining why it didn't work earlier. If you are entering a market that was tried unsuccessfully before, why is the situation different now?

And there are also approaches that are unhelpful.

- Recounting specific analyst research that supports the team. These slides beg to be challenged.
- Assuming that a current favorable trend will continue. Without noting underlying drivers, there is no reasoning that supports these claims.
- Answering "why us" instead of "why now." I see this in over 10% of weak examples. It's a sign that the presenters misunderstood the purpose of such a slide.

To make sure your own Why Now slide tells your story advantageously, write the slide only after going through the Why Now Session. Otherwise, you won't have the additional context needed to answer its challengers.

To evaluate a pitch that includes a Why Now slide, the easiest ways to test whether you should believe the story are to dive into the timing drivers, how they work, and how the business model could change. Otherwise, you will be operating without that needed context.

Thinking about timing is not just for your PowerPoint slides. It's also good for your own strategy.

How Early Should You Invest?

Think back to Andreessen's saying that it's more about "when and not if." If that's true and if there's not much cost of waiting, should we just invest early?

It's an interesting thought.

The challenge is that if you invest too early you might be forcing a not-good-enough product. But you might also be able to identify a niche where the product actually is good enough. One that gives you time to continue to develop the product, improve the business model, and expand to other niches.

There is another cost to entering early. Products built on outdated technology may never catch up with newer ones. Teams that jump in early and enter a not yet developed market also must be able to last long enough, potentially needing to raise more rounds of funding and with less progress to show than if they had entered later. Will the founders stay personally invested as their equity dilutes?

Where there's some predictability you might go for it. Of the timing drivers I listed, there is implied predictability in some examples, most famously in Moore's Law. It's not that it's a law of the universe that every 18 to 24 months we see a doubling of the number of transistors on a microchip but much of the industry is organized and committed to investment that helps that trend continue.

With that predictability you can "run Moore's Law in reverse," as Alan Kay says. Get the future benefits today. That lets you build and test with real customers now. Then, at an expected future date, the business model will work. As long as you can survive the initial building and testing period and can preserve those early customers, you'll be ahead.

That means that if you want the performance benefits of those future products today, you can have them. You just need to pay. And you need to pay beyond what makes the business model work.

Value created for your customers	>	Value captured by the business	<	Cost to provide the value
$$$		$		$$$

On the above model, costs are out of line with the other parts of the business model. But that can be a point of entrance for you if you know that those costs will decline along a workable timeline. In some cases you might enter like this, knowing that early customers will prove that the value actually is there, as long as you expect to deliver that value more cheaply later.

A bit earlier than the Xerox PARC example of running Moore's Law backwards was Bell Labs' definition of innovation as centered around sustainable business models.

"To an innovator, being early is not necessarily different from being wrong."[29]

But what too early is depends on the willingness of the organization to invest long term. If you can survive through the "too early" phase, you might be able to capture a market, establish standards, set the dominant design, or restrict access to potential competitors.

When Previous Bad Experience Means Ignoring Second Chances

The Why Now Session I described above includes looking at past failed products and companies.

In many cases, those past examples were small failures and mostly forgotten. But some of them became big failures that left investors and customers with a memorable negative experience.

That past experience then clouds new attitudes. People project forward with the belief that "We tried this before and it didn't work. If we try it again, it won't work either."

Instead we should ask: what has changed since we saw this concept last? Does our previous bad experience cloud our judgment for new opportunities in a different environment?

There are different types of this.

We see one type when investors have a bad experience with startups in a specific industry (meaning they lose a lot of money). Those same investors may be reluctant to invest in that same industry years later, even if the situation has changed. For example, after the Theranos failure, other blood testing companies faced closer scrutiny and even the question of how they could succeed when better-funded Theranos didn't.

We see another type when companies have a big failed product launch and then project another failure onto the next potential product. For example, this happened with AT&T's failed new video phone service in

1970 clouding their belief in the new market for cellular telephony. A 1971 AT&T study came to the conclusion that "there was no market for mobile phones at any price."[30] (This was different from the 1980s McKinsey study.) While the early 1970s was quite early for cellphone development, AT&T's practice of long-term investment might have saved them from abandoning the market too soon in the 1980s.

How Early Should You Build?

If preparing a little before an invention could become a financially sustainable innovation can be a path to success, how early should we build?

To answer that question requires estimating when the timing will be right. Some questions to ask:

- What new technological invention, if any, is required? Do we believe we can ride on top of other "laws" (or the work and investment of other industries) or do we need to develop those new technologies ourselves?

- Do we need to develop an ecosystem? Do we require new infrastructure?

- What switching costs do potential customers face? Is our product good enough for them to accept those costs? Or can we remove those costs through business model innovation?

- Can our team move quickly? Are we culturally suited to move fast, as early entrants, or slower, as later entrants? Either can be the appropriate answer. It depends on the organization.

The way Steve Jobs looked at this question included estimating which technologies are becoming ready to power their next products.

"The way we've succeeded is by choosing what horses to ride really carefully, technically. We look for these technical vectors that have a future and are headed up... Different technologies have their cycles: their springs and summers and autumn and winters... And so we try to pick things that are in their springs. And if you choose wisely, you can save yourself an enormous amount of work versus trying to do everything. And you can really put energy into making those new emerging technologies be great on your platform..."[31]

Having good timing usually isn't about a single point in time that is best. Instead, there are time ranges that may all be good and good for different reasons.

How do you choose when to enter? Let's go back to the timing chart we've used throughout the book.

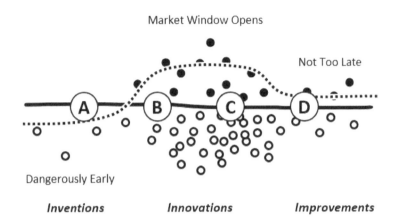

At time A, even though there are no strong timing drivers present and currently no sustainable business model, you believe that that will change. You also believe that both the timing drivers and business model will become favorable on a timeline that makes sense for you to start developing that potential product today.

Companies that take this approach especially benefit from timing drivers that are more predictable in nature, for example expected cost declines in supporting tech.

In other cases, founders know that they can pull the future forward by devoting resources to an opportunity earlier than others would.

At time B, you aim to enter when there are supporting timing drivers and a sustainable business model, but on the early side. You might make that decision for a few reasons.

Entering on the early side could work best if you can limit the access of competitors to needed resources, if you could influence the development of standards, if you believe you could delay competitors through intellectual property development and protection. Your organization might be stronger with new product development than marketing.

At time C, there are already early products in the new market. But you decide to enter a bit on the later side because you value watching what others do and then improving upon their mistakes. Your organization might be stronger with marketing than new product development.

At time D, there already are dominant players in the market. You choose to enter late, but as a niche product. The way to build the product is relatively clear, but versions of it haven't yet been deployed to your market niche. You understand that niche and can modify your product accordingly.

Depending on your situation, you might make arguments for any of those four points. It's up to you to decide when the time is right.

Timing Shifts the Market Size

In 2014, when Uber was a few years old and had a $17 billion valuation, Aswath Damodaran, a finance professor from NYU, wrote a detailed article on why that valuation was too high.[32] One of Uber's investors and board members, Bill Gurley, wrote a rebuttal.[33]

The basis for the rebuttal was that Uber's total addressable market (TAM) was not what Damodaran thought. Damodaran projected stable growth in market size – an assumption that worked for years in the past – using the slowly growing legacy taxi market. Meanwhile, Gurley projected that Uber would change user behavior and expand the overall market as people who previously would have taken taxis, public transportation, rented a car, walked, or stayed home, started to use Uber.

Damodaran estimated the 2014 global taxi and car-service market at around $100 billion and an assumed market growth rate of 6% per year. The question then was what share of that market Uber could win. To that, Damodaran gave an estimate of 10%.

But as Gurley explained in his response, "When you materially improve an offering, and create new features, functions, experiences, price points, and even enable new use cases, you can materially expand the market in the process. The past can be a poor guide for the future if the future offering is materially different than the past."

To compare, the below circle on the left represents the size of the market today. The circle on the right is the size of the market in five years, growing 6% per year. Compared to the left circle's present market, the future market on the right is 1.34 times the size.

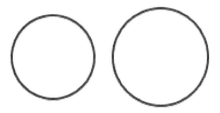

 But what about times when you see much faster growth? Uber, which in 2012 Gurley noted was growing at 20% per month (almost growing to 9x after a year), would see very different results.

Let's choose a more modest, though still fast-growing comparison: a company that grows 100% over a year.

The below circle on the left is the size of the market today. But the circle on the right is the size of the market in five years, growing 100% per year. Compared to the left circle's present market, the future market on the right is 32 times the size. As you can tell, I had to shrink the left circle so the right circle could fit on the page.

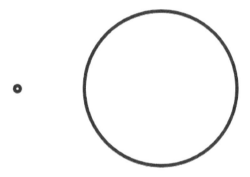

In San Francisco, one of Uber's first urban markets, it didn't take long for the company to grow larger than the entire existing number of private black cabs in the city.

A strong timing advantage can unlock value like that.

When you have a timing advantage, the world of the future stops looking like the world of the past. The world of the future also stops being a linear projection of the world of the past. Those expectations and stable projections are going to change.

100 years before Uber, when cars were only starting to become popular, they were sometimes seen as a fad. The number of horses in the US continued to grow until 1920. By 1927 there were as many cars in the US as horses. Cars continued to grow, while horses continued to decline.

The number of horses never went to zero, of course, but their use as a common means of transportation was over.

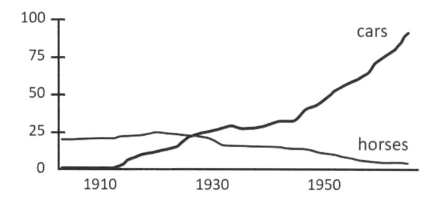

Population in millions. Source: Micromobility Industries, Horace Dediu

Imagine thinking through the timing exercise in the year 1890, four years after the first car was invented. How should we think through the market for horses?

"The car is a passing fad." Seen this way, horses in the economy would continue to grow with the population. There may be some benefits to breeding horses that are a better fit for local transportation, farm work, hauling heavy loads, war, and other specializations.

"Growth in rail travel, including local rail, means that more transportation may shift to rail." Horses will still play a major role in local transportation as they don't need to ride on rails and can maneuver difficult ground.

"Cars are only in the early stages of their development and can improve." If car travel improves as ships (sails to steam power) and land travel (animal powered to steam and petroleum powered) then their features may eventually make them better than horses.

Therefore, pitching a business that has a timing advantage means that those evaluating the opportunity (investors, board members, senior management, founders) need to understand why the market could grow.

You don't need that market to be large now. Instead, consider the small markets that could become big.

Too Early Examples

A big timing risk is being too early. How do you know if you may be too early?

There are different ways to approach this.

First, you may be too early in a good way. For example, predictable cost decline meant that it made sense for data storage-related products like Gmail and Dropbox to launch even before their user costs fell to a breakeven point. Your assessment of timing drivers may leave you confident with the probability that your needed capabilities will emerge on a timeline you can live with. You believe that the three parts of your business model will come together.

But if you lack any of those beliefs – if you're too early in a bad way – then stop. You may be the first mover but won't gain a first-mover advantage. Let a better-funded competitor that could lose money for years start first. Then enter when conditions are better.

History is full of examples of founders trying to bring products to market too early. We just often forget about these examples.

When I ask people they usually have no clear idea when the first version of a product came on market. Those early versions might have proved what was possible, but they didn't capture the market and for a number of reasons.

Here are some products, common today, that probably launched before you expected.

These products today are most commonly integrated into a single device, the modern smartphone.

- First mobile phone: 1946, priced at $15 per month plus $0.15 per minute (equal to $243/month plus $2.43/minute in 2024). Here I'm talking about the first mobile – not handheld – phone subscriptions. Those phones were installed in cars because size, weight, and power requirements made them too big for handheld use. You can watch demo videos of the technology put out by AT&T. Car phones became more popular by the 1970s - 1980s and handhelds followed soon after.

- First voice typing: late 1950s. This one is a bit of a cheat, because that specific technology was never commercialized. It was a school project by high school student Victor Scheinman, where by connecting his typewriter to a microphone and oscilloscope, he demonstrated the ability to speak a letter of the alphabet in order to trigger the typewriter to type the right key. Modern voice typing became popular in the early 2010s.

- First digital camera: 1975. See below for the story.

First Digital Camera

The inventor of the first handheld digital camera received the following advice: "That's cute, but don't tell anyone about it. That's how you shoot yourself in the foot!"

Everyone reading this has probably taken many pictures. Most of them are probably digital. But for the first 150+ years of the history of photography, people captured images physically and mostly on photographic film.

Two companies dominated film: Kodak and Fujifilm. But they dealt with emerging opportunities to move from film to digital in different ways.

Steven Sasson was a new engineer at Kodak when he developed the first digital camera in 1975. Sasson's digital prototype was big and bulky, though not out of line with an earlier generation of cameras. It weighed 8 pounds and had a 0.01 megapixel resolution. It took 23 seconds to record images to a cassette tape. Kodak never commercialized the technology.[34]

But over a decade after Sasson's prototype, Fujifilm did roll out a digital camera.

In 1988, shortly after introducing disposable cameras, Fujifilm released its first digital camera, the FUJIX DS-1P, and kept improving on it. A later version had 2 Megs of SRAM (static random-access memory) and could hold 5 to 10 photos. Compare that to a roll of 35mm film which typically held 24 to 36 exposures.

This is an example of two competitors taking different approaches to an emerging technology. One (Fujifilm), entered with digital products that could cannibalize their film business, but years before the products were ready for the mainstream (mostly because of cost and quality). And the other (Kodak) delayed its entry, until it was too late.

As a large company, Fujifilm could afford to invest for years until the timing was right. When digital cameras and smartphones became mainstream, Kodak's business suffered further until entering bankruptcy in 2012 (later reorganizing and expanding its offerings). Fujifilm is still going strong.

Many mention the Kodak digital story as a lost opportunity. But could Kodak have managed to switch its focus from film and chemicals to digital? 1975 was too early.

Timing in Different Markets

Your Market Type Impacts Your Timing Advantage

Steve Blank, author of *Four Steps to the Epiphany*, describes four market types that need different approaches to business building. What can we learn from these when it comes to timing?

Existing Market: This is a market where the problem, solution, customers, and producers are established. You most likely shouldn't compete directly with existing incumbents. Instead, you need to more deeply understand what existing customers need, whether their needs are being satisfied by incumbents, and what it requires for them to move to a new producer.

Resegmented Market: Here you go after the opportunity to slice an existing market in different ways rather than compete directly with existing producers, for example by becoming the low-cost producer or the niche producer.

New Market: Many of the examples in this book are for new markets. New markets are good in that they offer a new space for a business to grow and can improve customer lives. But new markets are challenging in that you may need to educate customers on why they need your product.

Clone Market: Clones take something that works in another geography and replicate it somewhere else in the world.

Timing works differently for each of them.

In **existing markets**, you need to be better, faster, or cheaper in order to enter. Drivers that enable those improvements will help you. Estimate the time by which you can access or build those improvements when your business model becomes sustainable because of those changes.

In some cases you may decide to launch "too early" here. That is, before the business model works. The reason being that when there is predictability in the timing of your new sustainable business model, you may decide to enter with a small project to learn, gain early adopters, or keep competitors out. That also lets you upsell or cross-sell those early customers later on.

Contributing drivers: technology, installed base, networks, distribution, and others.

Examples:

- AI-enabled app builders that make app creation faster and cheaper.

- Zoom entered the existing video communications market, but with no required signup or application install.

In **resegmented markets**, going cheaper becomes possible because of timing drivers. A high cost might come from technological, installed base, regulatory/legal, available talent, or distribution drivers. When those drivers are no longer a problem, you can resegment the market.

Going niche makes sense when that niche is profitable enough for you or when you believe it could grow into something significant for you.

Contributing drivers: similar to the above: technology, installed base, networks, distribution, but also social/behavioral and demographic.

Examples:

- Polaroid film and cameras to allow amateur photographers to see their photos after 60 seconds, with minimal training and no need to develop and print film.

- AI tools that specialize in their output. For example, the AI tools that serve the logo design market by generating cheap and immediate alternatives to graphic designers.

- MOOCs (massive open online courses) delivered education online, free or cheap, but without a degree. For people who wanted to learn cheaply but who didn't care about college prestige or a diploma, they are a relevant option.

In **clone markets** localize what worked elsewhere while taking advantage of the opening created by timing drivers.

This is sometimes just noticing a gap. That is, there is something new that's working in another part of the world or in another market. Expecting that customer demand will also exist in an unapproached market means that you can localize that product for another location.

And building a clone often also requires speed of execution. Someone else proved that a market exists elsewhere. Your belief is that you can duplicate their product in another location.

Contributing drivers: these are likely to be regulatory/legal drivers that remove a previous prohibition, a social/behavioral change, new distribution, or an economic change that supports the product in spite of an otherwise ignored market.

Examples:

- Lazada, which built Amazon for Southeast Asia. Zalando, a European clone of Zappos.

- Rocket Internet founded Wimdu, which cloned Airbnb. Here the clone also moved with speed. Wimdu had 10,000 apartments in 150 cities listed in under 100 days. Accoleo, 9flats, and others also cloned the Airbnb concept.

- As US-China tensions rose, Zoom (a US-founded company) went from being very responsive to demands from China's government to occasionally blocked in China. To fill that gap, Tencent launched its Voov videocall product. The user interface is almost exactly the same as Zoom's.

In **new markets**, your recognition of timing drivers helps you figure out what new capabilities exist. The question then becomes whether demand will exist once you create the product.

As Blank described above, you need to educate customers before they understand why they need your product. Another way to think about it is that if you see existing niche behavior, it may be a clue that this behavior could go mainstream.

Contributing drivers: Any drivers could impact this market, but especially social/behavioral, regulatory/legal, tech, installed base, networks, and crisis.

Examples:

- Dropbox changed user behavior from emailing or physically exchanging digital files to one where it was easy to share them online. Customers feared that Dropbox would view their files or that they would be corrupted. Those early customers had to be reassured that their files were safe.

- Motorola's DynaTAC was the first commercially available handheld mobile phone. As common as mobile phones are today, the companies that created the required technology around them doubted that they represented a significant market, believing that the market was limited to traveling salespeople and truck drivers.

Webmail vs Legacy Email

Hotmail was the first email service you could use right from a browser. In a few years, they gained over 8 million users and were acquired by Microsoft for $500M.

At the time of the Hotmail acquisition I worked for an officer of a public company that, among other things, sold legacy email services. She told me one day: "These free email services scare the hell out of me." That comment made sense for a company that over the past decade had charged a lot for email when few had access to the Internet. Those days were ending.

Not many remember, but the ways people accessed email in the 1990s were different from today. In the 1990s email users typically accessed email by dial-up from home, by dedicated line from work, or by dialing into a local Point of Presence (POP) phone number when traveling. Users downloaded email to their computers rather than looking at it online. Email was a paid service and sometimes priced by message size. I learned that when someone from the accounting department unexpectedly visited me to show me the internal cost of an email with a large attachment that I had sent to a group at work.

Users often could not set up multiple accounts without incurring extra costs.

But in 1995 Hotmail changed a lot of that. Hotmail was:

- Free to use, rather than paid.

- Without a limit on email addresses an individual could set up.

- Viewable in a browser from anywhere with Internet access rather than only by dialing into company-specific access points.

Hotmail's timing involved a few supporting drivers:

- Growing Internet access.

- Widespread use of web browsers as the main way people accessed the Internet.

- A growing market beyond business users.

- The potential to subsidize the service with ads as infrastructure costs fell.

But even on a free service like Hotmail, storage capped out at 2 Mb. Just seven years after the Hotmail acquisition, in 2004, Gmail offered 1 Gb of free storage, or 500 times more storage than Hotmail. By 2013, 15 Gigs became the norm. That was 7,500 times what Hotmail originally offered.

Of course, what had also changed was the cost of digital storage and bandwidth. What had been relatively expensive per Megabyte became cheap per Gigabyte. And what had been mostly text emails started to include images, video, and other large file formats.

In a Gold Rush Should You Sell Shovels?

There's an old saying, "in a gold rush, sell shovels."

The saying comes from an assessment that during the California gold rush of 1849, the people who got rich weren't the prospectors searching for gold, but instead were the ones selling equipment, clothing, and shovels.

It's a nice saying, but it is only partially true.

Thinking back to those old sellers of shovels, at least one of them is still well-known today. That's Levi Strauss, maker of the tough denim jeans gold miners wore. A less famous name from that time – Samuel Brannan – owned the general store at Sutter's Mill, where gold was discovered in 1848. Sutter's Mill became the target destination for many gold miners at the time. They stocked up on supplies at Brannan's store.

But is it always good advice to sell shovels? No. How do you know when you'd be better off selling shovels and when you'd be better off actually mining for the gold?

In the metaphorical gold rushes of the Dotcom bubble and the Telecom bubble, the early crypto or Web3 market, mobility, VR/AR, generative AI startups, and more, certainly some company founders (gold miners) did very well compared to the supporting services (shovel sellers).

Should you be Strauss, Brannon (different types of shovel sellers), or a gold miner?

Brannan did well with his general store. With the only store between San Francisco and the discovered gold deposits, Brannan was able to charge a markup of 75 times on the gold prospecting supplies he sold. Ultimately, when the miners left, his store lost its customers. He failed to maintain the business and he failed for personal reasons.

Strauss was able to sell his jeans and then scale the business way beyond gold miners.

Type 1: "General Store." These shovel types solve a need of high-demand customers, but with a product of local access. It's hard for others to enter this market (in the case of the store, a geographic market). It offers a non-mobile product that customers cannot carry elsewhere. *Establish the moat.*

Type 2: "Jeans." These shovel types solve a need of high-demand customers and offer a superior product compared to other offerings. Others can enter given technological capabilities. The product can spread easily, meaning that existing customers can carry the product to new markets. *Be the best option.*

Type 3: "Gold miner." These entrepreneurs have an insight that others lack and can act on it. They may have a superior technology and are able to invest as the timing advantage comes together, along with their passion and founder mentality. *Work on the right opportunity at the right time.*

Type 1: Organize an AI conference.

Type 2: Build a diagnostic tool targeted to AI companies.

Type 3: Develop a new AI tool targeted to financial advisors.

All could succeed for timing reasons.

When a Timing Advantage Requires an Ecosystem

In this book I've focused on products that are either simple enough to realize directly (like Airbnb) and avoided the complexity of products that required new ecosystems to support their popularity (like Tesla needing electric chargers stationed at convenient intervals).

But I want to briefly mention the lack of an ecosystem as a reason for timing failure and how that fits with timing.

There are numerous examples where a product could in theory have been created with market demand, but a nonexistent ecosystem prevented real success.

By ecosystem, I mean the network of complementary goods, services, partners, and activities necessary for the success of that product. This broader context is crucial for the successful adoption and sustainability of innovative products.

For instance, consider the case of Better Place, a company that aimed to revolutionize the electric vehicle (EV) industry. Better Place provided battery swapping stations, allowing EV drivers to quickly replace depleted batteries with fully charged ones. The concept required a widespread network of battery swapping stations, significant investment in battery technology, and coordination with car manufacturers to standardize batteries.

Better Place was extreme in what it required. The infrastructure for battery swapping stations was expensive and took years to develop. Car manufacturers resisted standardizing their battery designs.

While early in the history of automobiles, the ecosystem of roads, gas stations, service stations, and more took decades to develop, Better Place went bankrupt in just six years even though the company had raised $850 million.

Timing Brakes and Blockers

So far I've written about drivers of timing – identifying changes that influence your decision to develop a product or enter a market.

I also explained that if you don't have any strong timing drivers, you might consider working on something else, making sure you can survive long enough until the world caught up to you, or even working to cause the change you depend on.

Let's go into more detail on what can hold you back.

There are timing brakes – things that slow you down.

And there are timing blockers – things that prevent you from succeeding.

Of the list of 12 timing drivers, several can operate as brakes or blockers.

I've included this section because, just like a Why Now Session can help you estimate if your product will enter the market at the right time, assessing brakes and blockers can help you know what to avoid.

For example, we could have had widespread adoption of telemedicine years ago.

- The communications technology needed for live video consults was available since 2009 or earlier through WebEx, Skype, and others.

- The installed base of laptops with built in webcams was at critical mass since at least 2010 or five years earlier as a niche audience.

- The demand for additional medical care in remote areas was present for decades or more.

- There was demand for easier-to-access medical care that reduced travel time and waiting room time.

- Some cash-based healthcare services were already online in niches.

But there were blockers.

- Regulation did not allow telemedicine to be reimbursed comparable with in-person visits.

- Regulation limited how patient information could be shared online.

- There was some fear in the medical establishment that remote visits could damage their business model or send patients elsewhere.

Blockers like that keep you living in the past.

But then a crisis popped up. As COVID lockdowns prevented all but essential in-person doctor visits, regulations changed and finally allowed telemedicine as an option.

Before COVID, companies building telemedicine products couldn't have established themselves in the expectation of a pandemic with lockdowns. But once the COVID crisis was identified and lockdowns became common, it became more likely to expect a regulatory change. The blocker was lifted. If you happened to be offering telemedicine services or technology, or were able to move fast as the pandemic emerged, you were in a good position.

Here's a list of brakes and blockers and how they impact each timing driver.

Driver	Brake	Blocker
Technological	The needed tech is dominated by other industries.	The needed tech is controlled or prohibited.
Social/Behavioral	The belief that "It's just the way the world is."	"It's against our beliefs." "It's wrong." "We don't do that."
Regulatory/Legal	It's a gray area that others avoid.	It's illegal.

Installed Base	There are limitations to the installed base we depend on.	It's too costly to develop. It takes too much time to develop. It's controlled by device makers or app stores.
Crisis	Sudden impacts to any of these.	Sudden impacts to any of these. We can't move fast enough.
Economic	It's too expensive.	Recessions, where our market or product is harmed.
Networks	They are too costly to develop. They take too much time to develop.	We can't attain critical mass.
Distribution	Distribution is dominated by other products. It's too expensive to reach customers.	Distributing products of this type is not allowed.
Capital Access	This industry isn't hot and capital flows elsewhere. Capital is scarce.	This industry is not allowed access to funding. This industry previously burned investors and they avoid it now.

Organizational	People move in and out of the industry quickly and knowledge is lost. There is limited cross-industry knowledge sharing.	New structures that reduce founder and investor risk aren't allowed.
Available Talent	Talent is scared away from some kinds of work.	Not enough talent is produced.
Demographics	Certain markets are too small to build for.	Market demographics are not favorable to the business.

We see blockers in many parts of the world, but you might not need to respect them. Different from the telemedicine example is the way sharing economy companies like Uber, Lyft, Bird, and Airbnb navigated their own regulatory restrictions. Those tactics involved developing grassroots support, intentionally entering attractive markets that prohibited the businesses, and then influencing regulatory change municipality by municipality.

Those companies offered their products in regulatory gray areas and then used a combination of their customers' positive experience and lobbying to force regulatory change. That's a tactic you can use if you have raised lots of capital and can drum up popular support.

But you need to gain that grassroots support first. Once the above companies became well-known, municipalities also started to prepare for their arrival. I was in Hong Kong when the Airbnb team arrived to set up operations and I met the first members who worked out of a coworking space. Shortly thereafter, Hong Kong (having a strong real estate and hotel industry) prohibited Airbnb. The team moved to Singapore. There was never time for that grassroots support to emerge.

Why Didn't It Happen Back Then?

There are many potential timing advantages from history that seem puzzling. Why didn't people just do the obvious thing?

What seems obvious to us now may have actually been brakes or blockers that prevented the new products. Here are some examples.

Something that prevented long sea voyages was the effect of scurvy, a disease that we now know comes from a lack of Vitamin C. There was no known cure, though there were many ideas (including having sailors drink sea water). It wasn't until 1747 that James Lind, a British Royal Navy surgeon, applied the scientific method and gave pairs of sailors with six different daily treatments, one of which was two oranges and a lemon. Those who received the oranges and lemon recovered from scurvy. So why didn't his findings solve the navy's problem? It was mostly a lack of promotion and reluctance to abandon older medical beliefs, for which some blame Lind. After Lind's experiments, he published his results in a confusing treatise, which only included a few paragraphs on the citrus fruit cure. It took years to rediscover the knowledge. Only in 1795 did the British Navy start to make lemon juice mandatory on its ships.

Wheeled luggage seems like an obvious improvement to carrying heavy suitcases. All the needed parts of the product (uh, wheels and luggage) were there. But while wheeled luggage was developed multiple times, at least from the 1920s, it took until the 1980s for it to take off. For that delay we can blame airport and train station design, smaller than we're used to today, with many staircases, and porters to carry bags.[35]

This issue goes way back. Ancient Greeks invented a steam-powered device around 30 BC, called the aeolipile, which spun when water in a central container was heated to produce steam. The aeolipile was occasionally used to move devices in temples (after being fed offerings by visitors), but didn't continue development to other uses.

In contrast to attempts at curing scurvy and easily moving luggage, it doesn't seem that anyone tried to make the steam-powered aeolipile more than a novelty. Not until 1500 years later was there an attempt at steam-powered ships in Spain.

Timing Patterns

We introduced timing drivers and how they work. But what about when they combine? I normally find that there is some combination of timing drivers at play when companies have strong timing advantages.

Timing drivers can combine in repeatable ways. After observing many of these interactions, I decided to categorize them into Patterns. This section should help you evaluate more specific situations and give you some ideas. When reading these, think of how you might apply these patterns to your own product development.

Here's my partial list of patterns, in no particular order. You might browse this section for ideas. I'm not going to present every possible combination (which would leave us with thousands). I'm only showing some of the most common ones I've observed.

If you want to generate new concepts, combine a few random drivers and see what new product ideas that sparks.

For a growing list, visit https://startupsunplugged.com/.

The Hermit Crab

Contributing Drivers: Technology, Crisis, Economic, Capital Access

This pattern describes the way companies can crawl into the unused infrastructure of earlier companies. This unused infrastructure may exist because of previous overinvestment, new technology, or repurposing.

Examples:

- The availability of inexpensive dark fiber after the 2001 telecom bubble. WorldCom, ICG, Williams, and others sold off to Verizon, Level 3, Teleglobe, and others. That in turn helped future Internet companies gain access to plentiful and inexpensive bandwidth. (Overinvestment example.)

- Cable telephony companies such as Cablevision Systems, Comcast, Cox Communications, and Time Warner, used the existing coaxial connections into the home to launch voice services. (New capability example.)

- Hadrian acquired old manufacturing plants and updated them for their automated manufacturing business. (Repurposing example.)

The Unlocked Asset

Contributing Drivers: Technology, Crisis, Economic, Installed Base, Demographic

A known asset exists, but in a locked state. The asset is "locked" because accessing it would be too expensive, or not technologically possible.

Examples:

- Papyrus scrolls buried at Herculaneum that were formerly unreadable become readable because of new research, capabilities, and competitions. Artifacts deemed destroyed become priceless expansions of ancient learning.

- The Marcellus Shale formation in the Appalachian Mountain region formerly represented a huge oil deposit that was impossible to extract. Fracking capabilities enabled extracting the oil affordably, making the US the world's largest oil producer again.

The New Capability

Contributing Drivers: Technology, Installed Base

This pattern emerges when there are enough users of a new technology, system, or platform to enable companies to build on that new supporting base.

Examples:

- Mobility businesses (Uber, Lyft, Lime) required an installed base of GPS-enabled smartphones with enough processing power to handle turn-by-turn directions.

- Photo and video-based social networking (Instagram, Snap, TikTok) needed an installed base of smartphone users. Even better when the phones gained front-facing cameras.

Founders noticing this pattern see market white space open up through the work of others. Those mobility businesses didn't develop the underlying technologies they depended on. Those image-based social media companies didn't develop the smartphone cameras. But both types of business founders did benefit from the installed base already in place.

The Predictable

Contributing Drivers: Technological, Social/Behavioral

Patterns of this type rely on Technology that progresses with some level of predictability (like performance curve effects on processing power, cost, and more) and combines that with enduring Social/Behavioral needs. That means there's pent-up demand for a product and that demand increases as the product becomes faster and cheaper. The product's improvement comes from the Technological improvements while the demand comes from the Social/Behavioral side.

Examples:

- Feature-phone mobile telephony (Motorola, Philips, Nokia handsets) became affordable and good enough to replace fixed line telecommunications. The behavioral constant was that people want to communicate with friends, family, and colleagues even when they are away from their landlines. Mobile phones connect people to people, while landlines connect places to places, as Martin Cooper, the Motorola engineer who developed the first handheld cell phone, said.

- Online data storage (Dropbox, Box, GoogleDrive, Gmail) became cheaper on a predictable timeline. People had already dealt with storing lots of files on their own devices. Online data storage options enabled flexible access and sharing.

- Streaming user-generated video content (YouTube, DailyMotion) were enabled by broadband penetration, digital cameras, and falling data storage costs. People had grown accustomed to sharing videos of themselves.

The New Freedom

Contributing Drivers: Regulatory/Legal, Social/Behavioral,

These patterns depend on the scheduled progress of new regulations (like expiring patents) or changing beliefs that are expected to lead to other changes. These industries had been held back because of regulatory/legal issues in spite of latent demand.

Examples:

- 3D printing (MakerBot). When many 3D printing technologies came off patent that helped create a slew of new companies building 3D printers and offering related services. The tech wasn't new, but more startups gained legal access to it. That didn't mean that people wanted 3D printing. Many of those companies failed.

- Cannabis products (MedMen). As cannabis achieved legalization in some states and with a longer-term belief in full federal legalization, businesses sought to turn a gray market product into something legitimate. Companies raised hundreds of millions of dollars professionalizing cannabis products. MedMen built cannabis dispensaries with the thoughtfulness of "Apple stores" – the kind of place you could bring your grandparents. (But MedMen's founders committed fraud and the company tanked.)

- Tobacco (Philip Morris, Juul). As cigarettes fell out of favor in response to years of education, advertising campaigns, and health effects, substitutes popped up. Electronic cigarette technology became at first possible and then better designed as vape pens enabled smokers to puff on an unlit device and, with low amounts of smoke, get away with smoking indoors. Early vaping devices didn't go through the same regulatory approvals as other tobacco products.

The Clone

Contributing Drivers: Economic, Regulatory/Legal, Social/Behavioral, Capital Access, Demographics,

With some localization, what is already popular in one geographic market can gain popularity in a new place. The clone then localizes the business for a new market, based on local market readiness. Some clone types also benefit from domestic bans on foreign companies.

Rocket Internet was successful for a while by researching businesses that worked in one part of the world, finding people to localize the working concept, and then funding the copycat's rollout to other parts of the world.

- Clone examples (and what they cloned): Lazada (Amazon), Wimdu (Airbnb), Renren (Facebook), Alando (eBay), Zalando (Zappos), Zhihu (Quora), Beeconomic and many others (Groupon),
- Industry examples: Transportation, social networking, communication, housing infrastructure and more.
- Social examples: Associations, forms of government, religion, expectations about the role of individuals.

This pattern includes most drivers. The ones it does not include: technological, organizational, and available talent, are the ones most likely to cross geographic boundaries unless they are held back.

Cloning a successful business is not trivial, but it does remove some of the risk since the business model has already been validated elsewhere.

The Toy

Contributing Drivers: Technological, Social/Behavioral

This pattern occurs when we see the emergence of a new product that is not built for the serious legacy user. The early product is released and if people use it in its early state with minimal features and imperfect design then they will certainly want to use it later as it's improved.

Another way of thinking about this is in the context of "Crossing the Chasm," the book by Geoffrey Moore. Moore notes that early adopters behave differently and can help you uncover your first customers as well as what you need to change to sell to the later, more mature market. The question is how much of this niche behavior is a preview of behavior that the majority will later display.

Anytime a new tech or behavior is dismissed as a toy, there's a potential opportunity. It means that people have fun using it and the current solutions aren't yet great.

Another way of looking at this – what do people spend their free time doing?

Examples:

- Early hobbyist computers pointing to later personal computers.

- PDAs (personal digital assistants) pointing to later smartphone and utility apps.

- Early wired-in VR headsets pointing to later much improved wireless headsets.

- Early bulky drones pointing to small, easy-to-use ones.

The Removed Barrier

Contributing Drivers: Regulatory/Legal, Technological, Social/Behavioral,

This pattern can emerge when people are already awkwardly doing something that the product solves in a better way. There is existing demand but a barrier that blocks people from easily satisfying that demand. (See also the Timing Brakes and Blockers section.)

Examples:

- The complexity, fragility, and expense of old photographic techniques (though in demand) gradually being replaced by better options.

- Coinbase took the awkward early behavior of buying cryptocurrency in-person with cash or through other risky ways and made it a high-trust online transaction.

- Airbnb solved the problems with online payments and trust seen with Craigslist and Couchsurfing.

- Cannabis companies took illegal or gray market sales and benefitted as the drug became legalized in more locations. We'll see similar activity as payments, cross-state transportation, and online advertising for the drug opens up as well.

The System Shock

Contributing Drivers: Crisis, Any

A sudden, extreme change leads to a reaction. That reaction opens new opportunities.

Examples:

- COVID reduced in-person retail and increased online ecommerce and led to the popularization of remote work products like Zoom, and the possibility of telehealth products.

- Financial scandals from Enron, WorldCom, and Tyco led to more regulation and the requirement to monitor employee messages. A result was the development of messaging supervision products to help companies adhere to new regulations and to catch early problematic employee behavior.

The Unavoidable

Contributing Drivers: Demographics, Capital Access, Technological, Economic

Some changes, such as demographic ones, lead to predictable outcomes or risks. The child of today will later need a job, their own home, and retirement benefits. What happens when the shape of the demographic pyramid changes?

Examples:

- One Child Policy in China resulting in greater attention on children, their education, and related purchases.

- Population decline in parts of Europe and Japan. Empty villages and a declining tax base.

- Labor imports or development of devices to assist an aging population. The future needs to support a large aging population with fewer working-age people.

The Moral Urgency

Contributing Drivers: Social/Behavioral, Distribution, Capital Access,

Patterns of this type can grow quickly and powerfully but it is not clear how long their support will last before being replaced by something else. Businesses that want to benefit from this pattern must quickly gain investment and lock in future commitments. That means that this pattern most benefits those who are either coincidentally already positioned to benefit before the pattern emerges or those business opportunities that can be built quickly. Or, those without morals who latch onto the trend and use social pressure and advantageous sales processes to win.

That generally means that simpler responses – things like pressuring people to allocate resources differently, rather than developing something new – work best here.

Examples:

- Post September 11th support for affected families, as well as for funding and educational opportunities for people in Afghanistan.

- Protests against racism leading to investments in minority-owned businesses.

- Climate change related product support, regardless of the product's actual climate impact.

The Psychological Barrier

Contributing Drivers: Social/Behavioral,

These examples are a bit different from the rest. Here I'm including human breakthroughs, rather than new products.

The concept is that we're kept from some breakthroughs because we believe they're not possible.

But be careful with this one. Some of the most famous examples are fake. But even these fakes can spark ideas.

Contributing Drivers: Social/Behavioral,

Examples:

- People like us, of our culture, of our religion, who went to our school, with our type of background... we just don't do this.

  These people certainly could include those with the capability or interest to create some specific breakthrough, but they don't think of it, choose not to, or are embarrassed to.

- A new way to compete in the high jump. Dick Fosbury created the "Fosbury Flop," a new way to do the high jump. It might be surprising, but earlier high jumpers went over the bar forwards using the straddle technique. Then along came Dick Fosbury, who in 1968 went over the bar backwards. With a cushioned fall, different jump styles were possible earlier. But people just didn't jump that way. Even after he debuted the Fosbury Flop it took years before it became the standard form. A few years after its introduction, all high jump record holders used the Fosbury method.

Here again, it's important to note that while Fosbury's method became the new norm, it led to slight, not dramatic, improvements in height. But that was enough.

A fake example (what you'll often hear):

- Breaking the four-minute mile. Roger Bannister was the first person to run a mile in under four minutes. That four minute barrier was there long enough that some people even believed it was impossible. Now we talk about the "Bannister Effect," or the phenomenon where someone shows that something believed impossible is actually possible, followed by many others achieving that formerly impossible goal.

  While Bannister's mile record may be used as an example of a psychological barrier, there's also a reinterpretation of the meaning behind his record. Before his 1954 race, the record for the mile stood at just over four minutes (4:01.4) for nine years. While speed records were set during WWII, they were all set by Swedish runners (Sweden being neutral in the war). The record today, which has stood since 1999, is 3:43.13. It's not a round number, so as a result gets less attention. Maybe that's why we don't think of it as a psychological barrier.

  I include this extra detail as a warning to be careful with this pattern. You may see barriers where none exist.

The Analog to Digital

Contributing Drivers: Technology, Social/Behavioral, Regulatory/Legal, Distribution,

There is still quite a lot of analog that could be transformed into digital.

Reasons for the transformation include cost (no cost to create additional copies of a digital product, unlike producing another physical copy), accessibility (no cost to distribute a digital product, unlike shipping a physical copy), and new forms of use (ability to edit and search digital copies, unlike static physical copies).

Examples:

- The original requirement for doctors to keep paper records, followed by the new mandate to move to Electronic Medical Records (or pay a fine), plus the human desire to avoid change at the end of a career.

- In-person educational instruction and assessment moving to online content delivery and assessment.

- Paper books giving way to e-readers, like the Kindle and Kobo, or just digital versions of the books themselves.

- Vinyl records and CDs giving way to digitally recorded music and streaming.

Streaming Music

Music streaming services popped up in the early 2000s, after Napster's rise and fall. These were often supported through audio ads, both to operate the business and to compensate the artists.

Then a friend told me about a free music streaming service that only ran image ads. No audio ads to disrupt your listening. This service was called Grooveshark and was founded in March 2006.

Grooveshark was like a cloud version of Napster. Users uploaded their music to Grooveshark for others to stream, rather than download to their computers.

Grooveshark was special at the time. You could use it internationally where other services were limited. The catalog was broad. And, most importantly, it was free and without audio ads. That meant that it kept playing without the interruptions so common in the other free services.

But Grooveshark ignored the needed licensing agreements for distributing copyrighted music.

And one day, Grooveshark was gone. They posted this message on their website:

> *"Dear music fans,*
>
> *Today we are shutting down Grooveshark.*
>
> *We started out nearly ten years ago with the goal of helping fans share and discover music. But despite [the] best of intentions, we made very serious mistakes. We failed to secure licenses from rights holders for the vast amount of music on the service.*

That was wrong. We apologize. Without reservation.

As part of a settlement agreement with the major record companies, we have agreed to cease operations immediately, wipe clean all the data on our servers and hand over ownership of this website, our mobile apps and intellectual property, including our patents and copyrights.

At that time of our launch, few music services provided the experience we wanted to offer -and think you deserve. Fortunately, that's no longer the case. There are now hundreds of fan friendly, affordable services available for you to choose from, including Spotify, Deezer, Google Play, Beats Music, Rhapsody and Rdio, among many others.

If you love music and respect the artists, songwriters and everyone else who makes great music possible, use a licensed service that compensates artists and other rights holders. You can find out more about the many great services available where you live here: http://whymusicmatters.com/find-music.

It has been a privilege getting to know so many of you and enjoying great music together. Thank you for being such passionate fans.

Yours in music,

Your friends at Grooveshark"

But for all of Grooveshark's problems caused by its founders skirting copyright law, the company was founded at a good time.

As a comparison, Spotify was founded in April 2006, just one month after Grooveshark.

Bad Patterns

Tackling the "Why Now" subject leaves us exposed to hindsight bias. As a result, I want to make sure that I also show examples where people thought that they were entering or exiting the market at the right time but were ultimately proved wrong.

Earlier in the book I quoted investor Roelof Botha, an astute observer of timing advantages and someone who acted on his interpretations by investing.

In his YouTube memo, Botha wrote: "Digital video recording tech is for the first time cheap enough to mass produce and integrate into existing consumer products, such as digital photo cameras and cell phones, giving anyone the ability to create video content anytime, anywhere. As a result, user-generated video content will explode."

He was so right about YouTube in 2005, but 10 years later in 2015, he was so wrong about VR reaching its moment.

As he wrote in TechCrunch in 2015:

"For the last 20 years VR has been just around the corner, but there have been three major hurdles in the way to mainstream adoption. Today, all three hurdles have been removed."[36] The hurdles mentioned were price, content, and fragmentation for production and distribution.

But VR ended up disappointing many who thought that it would indeed have its breakout year in 2016.

How can we protect ourselves from falsely assessing that the time is right?

We might just limit our exposure to our decision. Rather than go all in, we might hedge our bets.

We can look for ways that others mistakenly believed they had identified that the time was right.

And we should also avoid traps where we convince ourselves without really thinking about potential outcomes.

In his YouTube memo Botha also outlined problems with video that existed in 2005. Files were too large to email, too large to host, there was no standardization of file formats, and videos existed as isolated files without interaction between viewers or interrelation between videos. But unlike the later VR example, video was already a big market. People were already viewing, recording, and sharing their own videos, just not very well. VR was much more niche and required an installed base of headsets that had not reached a critical mass.

To give you ideas, here are some false Why Nows to consider.

The Wrong Curve

Contributing Drivers: Any

As Yogi Berra said: "It's tough to make predictions, especially about the future." When we make a prediction based on our current understanding we can fall into traps.

Or, taking Marc Andreessen's quote from the start of the book literally – that there are no bad ideas, only ideas whose time has not yet come – the Wrong Curve Pattern suffers from a misjudgment of the speed of change.

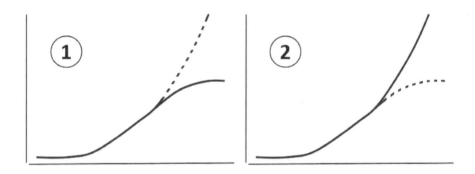

In Type 1, what seems to be improving on an exponential curve instead flattens into S-Curve. The needed improvements are still years away. Early companies shut down or burn cash seeking the improvements they need to bring their product to market.

Type 2 occurs as the opposite of the above. What seems to be an S-Curve instead turns into an exponential curve. Companies are convinced that early products aren't promising and exit, only to see the market grow soon afterward.

Examples:

- Type 1: Autonomous Vehicles. In 2015 it was common knowledge that AVs would be widely available by 2020. For example, Starsky Robotics focused on autonomous trucking, which looked promising, but shut down in 2020. From their founder, Stefan Seltz-Axmacher:[37]

  > *"Timing, more than anything else, is what I think is to blame for our unfortunate fate. [T]he space was too overwhelmed with the unmet promise of AI to focus on a practical solution. As those breakthroughs failed to appear, the downpour of investor interest became a drizzle…. Back in 2015, everyone thought their kids wouldn't need to learn how to drive. Supervised machine learning (under the auspices of being "AI") was advancing so quickly — in just a few years it had gone from mostly recognizing cats to more-or-less driving. It seemed that AI was following a Moore's Law Curve…. Rather than seeing exponential improvements in the quality of AI performance (a la Moore's Law), we're instead seeing exponential increases in the cost to improve AI systems — supervised ML seems to follow an S-Curve."*

  We've certainly seen other breakthroughs in AI since that quote from 2020. We'll see how fast fully autonomous vehicles come on market and the way companies deal with the regulatory, social/behavioral, and other related drivers.

- Type 2: AT&T's divestiture from mobile. In 1985, McKinsey Consulting's research determined that there was a limited market for cell phones (probably just traveling salespeople and truck drivers). After thousands of customer surveys they estimated that mobile subscriptions wouldn't even reach one million by the year 2000. Therefore, AT&T should exit the market. The actual number of mobile customers in 2000 ended up being over 100 times as many. AT&T later bought its way back into mobile at many times the price it had sold.

When do we see exponential curves or S-curves? Think through these questions.

What are the related resource constraints? What will prevent us (or our product) from continuing to grow? Are we going to run out of a required resource?

Do we face market share saturation? What kind of adoption curve might we see? On what timescale?

Constraints and negative feedback loops can lead to S-curves. We can see exponential curves when we lack those constraints or have positive feedback loops.

The Oversold Utopia

Contributing Drivers: Social/Behavioral, Demographics,

When there is a lot of money already raised and more to be made, the incentive is to tell the utopian story of how the world will be great when the invented products are mainstream.

- Type 1 is where new products seem so different and kindle such imagination, that their creators believe they will end war.

  This belief has occurred multiple times, including with the telephone, dynamite, radio, submarines, and more. The belief comes from a couple origins.

  There was the positive – the telephone would make communication so easy that differences across distance would disintegrate.

  And then there was the negative – that dynamite would make war so horrific that no one would dare fight.

- Type 2 is similar to the above, but instead of unbridled optimism it's the rosy picture that founders put on their companies and investors put on their investments. You must be able to assess who stands to benefit if the stated future comes true.

  Included here are the ways that rideshare companies dismissed critics with claims that their companies reduce traffic and are good for the environment. Traffic actually increased. And lots of bikes and scooters ended up cluttering streets and sidewalks, in addition to landfills.

  Homeshare companies dismissed critics as being against renters making extra money when the practice can also make it harder for residents to find full-year leases and can lead to increased rental rates overall.

- In Type 3, we're intentionally misled by people fabricating progress. The lessons here are from years and billions invested in fraud-ridden companies, among other examples.

113

Without knowing better we might make plans based on these fake results.

An outsized example of this is blood testing company Theranos' fabrication of test results. The team fooled a lot of experienced people who either didn't do their own research or didn't want to believe the criticisms they heard. A more accounting-style version comes from the FTX fraud.

The Illusion of Immediacy

Contributing Drivers: Technological, Social/Behavioral, Capital Access

The Illusion of Immediacy Pattern arises when there is a false perception that the market is ready for the rapid and immediate adoption of a new technology or product. This pattern is often driven by overestimating the readiness of both the technology and the market, leading to premature launches and investments.

The difference between this and the other Bad Patterns is the dependence on market demand.

The 2016 VR example I gave at the beginning of this chapter was one of these. There are many more.

- E-Commerce in the Early 2000s. During the initial surge of the Internet, many believed that the majority of retail would swiftly shift to ecommerce. This belief led to a rush of investment in online retail startups. However, it took more time for Internet penetration to become almost total and for consumers to trust online transactions. Even in the years after the COVID pandemic (when there was a jump in online retail) sales penetration was still around 20% in the US. Many early ecommerce ventures failed because the market wasn't ready as quickly as they expected.
- Wearable Technology. Initially, there was a strong belief that wearable technology, particularly smartwatches and fitness trackers, would rapidly become indispensable to consumers. While the market grew, it did so more slowly than many predicted. Beliefs in immediate market adoption led to early entrants struggling to survive the slower pace of consumer adoption.
- 3D Television. In the early 2010s, there was a strong push by manufacturers and content providers towards 3D television, anticipating it would be the next step in home entertainment. Despite the technological advancements and significant

investment, 3D TV failed to gain widespread acceptance. The reasons included the need for special glasses, lack of content, and consumer indifference towards the 3D experience in a home setting. 3D TV products were discontinued as of 2017. The intriguing difference now (as of 2024) is that 3D TV is predicted to make a comeback, especially due to sports content in the format. But as I wrote earlier, just beware of analyst reports.

In all these cases, the common theme is the misjudgment of the market's readiness for a new technology or product. The Illusion of Immediacy bad pattern can lead to significant financial losses and strategic missteps. It underscores the importance of accurately assessing not just the technological capabilities but also market readiness and consumer behavior. Avoiding this pattern requires not overinvesting up front.

Does Focusing on Timing Devalue Founders?

Doing this research I've met two types of people.

One type are those who agree that timing is important and who, depending on their work, try to take timing into account in their product, investment, or other decisions. Some of them even read my earlier drafts, participated in workshops, or brought me in for discussions.

But there's a second perspective people have. That's where they feel that timing is not a big factor in the success of a product. Some go so far as to say that timing is a meaningless – even a defeatist – approach to take. That is, looking at the way timing works and its impact removes the role of the founder in bringing forth their vision. There's no founder agency at play.

I don't claim any of that.

Founders absolutely change the world.

But founders often successfully change the world when they also happen to be supported by timing drivers.

Of the two types above, the second has a dangerous side in overreliance on the Great Man Theory of history. Yes, the world was different because there was a Thomas Jefferson, a Lee Kuan Yew, and a Napoleon Bonaparte. As well as Thomas Edison, Henry Ford, and Steve Jobs. Though all of those founders could be viewed as beneficiaries of good timing. If their environment had been different, maybe they would not have become great. Or maybe they would have focused on different activities and found greatness in a different arena.

And if the first type above over-relies on timing, then it can lead to a low agency view of the world. A belief that people behave like uniform molecules in a solution.

In recent years, more people seem to have become uncomfortable with the idea that great individuals can produce great changes. They are wrong – individuals who have a vision, capability, and who care enough to work for it absolutely do change the world.

Just don't dismiss the first type: that if you want to make great change you should work on a problem whose time has come.

Steve Jobs, interviewed in 1994 by the Santa Clara Valley Historical Association said:

"Life can be so much broader, once you discover one simple fact, and that is that everything around you that you call 'life' was made up by people who were no smarter than you. And you can change it, you can influence it, you can build your own things that other people can use. Once you learn that, you'll never be the same again."[38]

That's Not What I Said!

"Everything that can be invented has been invented."

That's a supposed quote from Charles Duell, Commissioner of the United States Patent Office from 1889 - 1901. As a result, Duell also supposedly recommended closing the patent office.

But there is no evidence of this quote.

And in 1902 Duell was actually quoted as saying: "In my opinion, all previous advances in the various lines of invention will appear totally insignificant when compared with those which the present century will witness. I almost wish that I might live my life over again to see the wonders which are at the threshold."[39]

What a shame to be best known for a quote contrary to your own beliefs.

Execution Risk vs Market Risk

Once you realize that "life" was made up by other people, you have to choose what to work on. Assessing timing will help you do that.

While I didn't include much discussion of non-timing related ways founders, investors, and teams fail, there are two types of risk I'll briefly mention: execution risk and market risk.

Execution risk is when you understand customer demand but find it tough to deliver value or outperform existing options. Market risk is when we overestimate how much demand there is for a product. We might build something amazing to an audience of no one.

On the execution side, because of timing drivers, it becomes possible to deliver new value, but can the team actually deliver? Or will another team win out instead?

For example, early social media services that demonstrated the possibility of online connections, only to lose out to other entrants. Founders at Columbia and Stanford built CU Connect and InCircle before Harvard had TheFacebook. Those earlier entrants failed to execute as well, including making poor decisions on design and funding.

On the market risk side, some products make sense only when they finally appear. In the world before these products, no one was calling for them, but when they became possible and available, demand followed. But that means we can also be wrong in the other direction, building products few people want.

For example, failed personal juicer startup Juicero raised $120M, but only sold a few thousand units, even after cutting prices. Not only was the market for expensive juicers not very big, the machines were overengineered, wouldn't work without wifi, and company juice packets could be squeezed by hand.

Streaming Music in the 19th Century

"The trouble with these beautiful, novel things is that they interfere so with one's arrangements. Every time I see or hear a new wonder like this I have to postpone my death right off. I couldn't possibly leave the world until I have heard this again and again."

That's a quote from Mark Twain in 1906, speaking about listening to music through the telephone, a product delivered by the Telharmonium.

There were even earlier signals that there was a market for such a thing. Other systems, including the théâtrophone, first demoed in 1881, which counted Victor Hugo and King Luís I of Portugal as customers, and a Budapest, Hungary service called Telefon Hirmondo, which offered everything from news, music, an events calendar, and commercials. The later Telharmonium service focused on music by

---

phone, starting in New York City in 1906.

The early music streaming businesses had problems in that they required power-hungry equipment that generated cross-talk on phone lines. The Telharmonium also required musicians to perform the music live rather than playing pre-recorded options, which were too low quality at the time.

Apart from technology problems, the Telharmonium was priced at $0.20/hour (equal to $6.60/hour in 2024). The tech was even less scalable than it seemed because the high electric power needed to transmit the music across early low fidelity phone wires meant that just generating the needed electricity was a significant cost. That fact also prevented a Telharmonium location in New York City from being able to offer service far from its location. That's to say nothing of the lack of long-distance calling back then. The business shut down in 1916.

Recorded music and home radio started to become popular in the 1910s and 1920s. Had something prevented radio and recorded music from emerging, would the Telharmonium have had a chance?

Steam-Engine Time

What other observations support the importance of timing?

Unless you believe in a silent, invisible ether that connects humanity, you have to admit it's curious when unconnected people around the world invent the same thing at nearly the same time.

There are many examples of this.

Could timing be behind these simultaneous inventions?

Here's a short list of some of the simultaneous inventions noted by William F. Ogburn and Dorothy Thomas in their 1922 paper *Are Inventions Inevitable? A Note on Social Evolution.*[40]

- Microscope. Claimed by Johannides, Drebbel and Galileo (1610?).
- Photography. Daguerre-Niepce (1839) and Talbot (1839).
- Electric motors. Dal Negro (1830), Henry (1831), and McGawley (1835).

- Microphone. Hughes (1878), Edison ((1877-78), Berliner (1877) and Blake (1878).
- Telephone. Bell (1876) and Gray (1876).
- Printing telegraph (like it sounds, a telegraph that prints typed words). Wheatstone (1845) and Bain (1845).

But maybe this inevitability only occurs with product inventions? What about scientific discoveries?

Here's another list from Ogburn and Thomas.

- Theory of the infection of microorganisms. By Fracastoro (1546) and Kircher.
- Nature of the cataract. Brisseau (1706) and Maltre-Jan (1707).
- Function of the pancreas. Purkinje (1836) and Pappenheim (1836).
- Form of the liver cells. Purkinje (1838), Heule (1838) and Dutrochet (1838).

The simultaneity of those examples could come from underlying research supporting the new discovery. A knowledge timing driver.

This simultaneous invention phenomenon is sometimes referred to as "steam-engine time," from a quote by the science fiction author Charles Fort in his 1931 book titled *Lo!*

"If human thought is a growth, like all other growths, its logic is without foundation of its own, and is only the adjusting constructiveness of all other growing things. A tree cannot find out, as it were, how to blossom, until comes blossom-time. A social growth cannot find out the use of steam engines, until comes steam-engine-time. For whatever is supposed to be meant by progress, there is no need in human minds for standards of their own: this is in the sense that no part of a growing plant needs guidance of its own devising, nor special knowledge of its own as to how to become a leaf or a root."[41]

From experience of similar environments and awareness of the same supporting timing drivers, people will notice the same opportunities.

But we need to remember that there is a difference between invention and innovation.

Are scientific inventions deterministic as earlier claimed?

That is, do inventions come out at the same time because there is enough supporting knowledge and it becomes inevitable that someone makes the discovery? That could be a reason why we see so many simultaneous inventions.

Or, are the simultaneous inventions a matter of chance? Dean Simonton and others made this argument.

Looking at data from the simultaneous inventions listed by several sources, researchers concluded that the frequency of simultaneous inventions fits a statistical distribution (the Poisson distribution). That would mean that we could see multiple inventors for all sorts of things just from chance.

But what do Simonton and others agree makes an invention more likely to happen? The number of people working on the problem. There, at least, is something deterministic about the rate at which these inventions should come about.

And a few of the timing drivers are related to just that point:

- Regulatory / Legal (are you allowed to work on the topic).
- Social / Behavioral (the topic is hot or taboo).
- Available Talent (related to the number of people working on a problem).
- Capital Access (financial support for the work).
- Crisis (temporary attraction to working on the topic).

We also have to remember when it comes to timing we're more interested in sustainable business models (innovation) than invention.

Many of the "too early" examples in this book failed because of their weak business models. It was technically possible to produce the thing, but it produced too little value, the business couldn't capture enough value, and the costs were too high.

To go back to the natural world examples, a product exists in an environment that helps or prevents its propagation.

In the book *Sleeping Beauties: The Mystery of Dormant Innovations in Nature and Culture*, Andreas Wagner recounts the history of many species which appeared before the earth was beneficial for them. In some of these cases it took tens of millions of years for the species to spread.

As an example, grasses eventually became the globe's dominant species 40 million years after they originated. According to Wagner, grasses "innovated" a few survival techniques that would later lead to their success, including being able to grow even after grazing animals ate their shoot tips and resistance to drought.

But Wagner explains that it wasn't grasses' innovations that destined them for greatness. Greatness here is defined as growth in numbers or radiation into many species. Instead, it was the earth's changing climate that did the trick. As the earth's continents changed shape, they formed broad dry regions where grasses had an advantage.

Another evolutionary history Wagner relates is that while mammals first appeared 225 million years ago, long before the dinosaurs went extinct, it took other environmental changes for them to branch into the over 5000 species on earth today. The growth and spread of mammals also benefited from the extinction of the dinosaurs, the emergence of flowering plants, and climate changes.

As a closing thought, what capabilities does your business, product portfolio, or potential investment have, that once the world is ready, would become advantageous? What needs to be true for you to win?

Summing Up

We covered a number of ways to understand timing and its effect on product success.

Timing work is not about trying to predict the future, but about being prepared for changes in domains that affect your work. You choose what to build and use the guidance from your perspective on when to build it.

A brief summary of the topics covered:

Look For Timing Drivers

Go through the list of timing drivers I provided. Which ones are relevant in your situation? What would you add to the list? How would you make the drivers more specific to your situation? How do you expect these drivers to change?

Run a Why Now Session and Build Timing Maps

To bring discipline to your thought process, work through a Why Now Session and build the related Timing Maps.

This is one of the formats I developed while workshopping the timing topic with businesses. To try it yourself, follow the example in the Why Now Session chapter. Look at the steps as outlined in the Appendix.

Add Your Business Model

Remember that without a financially sustainable business model (or one that will eventually become sustainable), you don't have a true timing advantage.

Depending on money raised or your budget, you might be able to work with an out of balance business model, but your timing perspective should point you to believe that the business model will become sustainable on a timeline you can accept.

Remember that inventions are not innovations until they have a sustainable business model.

Market Size Can Radically Change

Don't only look for large markets that exist today. What formerly seemed to be a non-existent, slowly growing, or small market can come into existence, grow quickly, and become large.

Timing advantages can have that outcome.

Brainstorm Patterns

Read through the list of Why Now Patterns. Learn from other examples and brainstorm helpful combinations of timing drivers.

Founders Create the Future

People dedicated to seeing their vision become reality can accelerate the change we see in the world. They devote their time and effort to initiatives that would otherwise never be accomplished.

Believing that timing is important doesn't remove founder agency. But founders are best off choosing what to work on and *when*.

Learn from History

In the book I provided examples of well-known and obscure products. There are many more. I will keep a running list on StartupsUnplugged.com.

Appendixes

Running the Why Now Session

Earlier I showed how to run a Why Now Session using YouTube as an example. Here's the list of steps to take.

You can run this exercise in a few ways and I recommend each step in the following order. I also included suggested time allotments and team member involvement. This is based on past experience running these workshops.

Steps and time needed:

- Form the team for the Why Now Session. That's the founders for early-stage startups, CXOs for later-stage, the product team for larger entities, the deal team for investors.

- Form the team for the "Challenge Session." These are the people who will try to pick apart your reasoning. The team could be made up of colleagues and friends for early-stage startups, colleagues across and outside the organization for later-stage startups, product leaders for larger entities, and partners or directors for investment teams.

- Run the Why Now Session (advance preparation plus 1 - 2 hours of live meeting time).

- Map the results of the Why Now Session to your business model (15 minutes).

- Share findings with the Challenge Team. This can be either live (15 minutes) or sent in advance for individual review.

- Run the Challenge Team Session. Present and take questions (1 hour total, with only 15 minutes for presenting and the rest of the time spent on questions).

Now let's run through each step for the session.

1) Go through the list of drivers. Which drivers are most important to your business now?

   If you end up with a long list, narrow down to the most important ones. Start to list the information relevant to your Why Now.

What relevant history should you know about? What earlier attempts were there at similar products?

What future expectations do you have? What will change because of the drivers you identified?

2) Draw your own rough diagrams based on the drivers, using the ones below as examples. Since your situation probably includes multiple drivers, draw these however it's most helpful to tell the story of what has changed or is changing. To keep your work readable, create a separate diagram for each driver. For example:

   ○ If your Why Now depends on a new technology becoming faster and cheaper, what's the expected timeline to reach the speed or cost you require?

   ○ If your Why Now depends on a new social/behavioral norm, when did it become a noticeable niche? How big does that niche need to be for a sustainable business opportunity?

3) Build what I call "Timing Maps." Put each relevant driver on its own timeline and show examples of the changes. Mark "today" at a spot that gives you enough room for the earlier examples.

4) If you have examples of earlier companies that tried similar ideas, place them on a timeline. If you're not sure, use the advanced search tools in Google and set a custom range for the years you want to search. What happened to those earlier examples? Did they fail because of bad timing?

5) If there are current companies building similar solutions, place them on another timeline, as below.

6) Now that you have done the above, mark these next points on your timelines:

   ○ The latest point at which you believe you would still be so early that your business would fail mainly because of timing. When were the drivers too weak to matter?

   ○ You can also draw a second line where you feel the market window will close based on how fast things are changing. This is where you expect other companies will dominate the industry if you don't act. Being too late may be less of a problem than being too early.

Drivers may operate on different timelines. I break them out separately and then stack them up to show the overall picture.

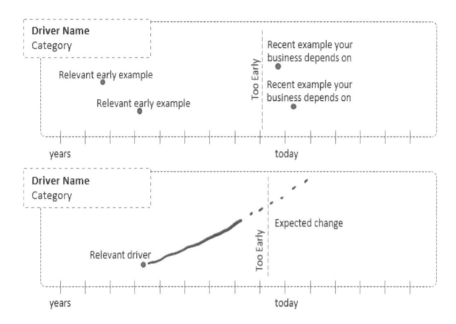

Also, some of these diagrams are loosely defined. When you do this exercise, it's going to show your perspective, not a single true or false answer. You do however need to back up your perspective with examples and data.

After this exercise, you can present all of this detail in a single slide when you pitch for investment or resources. But the result of this exercise is that when you do speak about your business and its timing benefits, you'll be able to have a much deeper discussion about your perspective.

Business Model Impact

Given the timing advantage you expect, what changes about the business model?

Importantly, for a financially sustainable business, those three parts must differ in magnitude in the following way.

| Value created for your customers | > | Value captured by the business | ≥ | Cost to provide the value |

After your Why Now Session and Timing Maps, describe what your new business model is (or will be). How do the three parts of the business model work together? Was the old business model unsustainable, where the new one is sustainable?

Evaluating Your Why Now

To truly benefit from changing timing drivers, those drivers must improve your business model in some way.

Here are the 12 timing drivers, with their potential impact on the three parts of a business model. This chart shows general areas of impact. When you go through this exercise, input specifics, including numbers, into your new business model.

Timing Driver	Value Created	Value Captured	Cost to Provide Value
Technological	Better performance: faster, smaller, cheaper, less energy intensive; leads to increased value.	Businesses can charge more because of higher performance, though this may be competed away.	Cost reduction for similar performance.
Social / Behavioral	New ways to satisfy enduring behaviors. New behaviors that need to be fulfilled.	More desire for your products.	Could go either way.

Regulatory / Legal	With liberalized regulatory or legal control, more products can be offered. Barriers to value provision (keeping others out).	What was previously blocked becomes permissible.	Could go either way.
Installed Base	Getting to market faster and cheaper because of the installed base built by another entity.	Monetizing the installed base, but for a new product.	Lower costs.
Crisis	Sudden change produces higher value for business.	Ability to capture more value because of a new need or extra demand for an existing need.	Often higher costs.
Economic	More/less disposable income leads to more/less willingness to pay higher prices.	Ability to charge more.	Rising costs.
Networks	More connections increase value.	New value is captured because of the network.	Networks require maintenance.

Distribution	Customers gain access to new products.	Larger markets to sell to.	Lower costs for similar delivery time and quality.
Capital Access	Creation of products that are not otherwise possible. More economic activity for businesses that require funding.	Build faster and bigger.	Economies of scale. Wasteful spending.
Organizational	Organizational learning leads to greater value produced.	More value produced can lead to more value captured.	Lower production costs.
Available Talent	Capability and creativity in producing new value. More producers extend existing business models to more customers.	Greater productivity.	Possibly lower costs per unit of output. Possible higher human capital costs.
Demographic	Market needs.	Changing market size. Niches to sell to.	Economies of scale.

Questions to Ask About Timing Drivers

When you consider each timing driver, what questions could you ask to test whether it impacts your situation?

In some cases, it might be obvious which drivers have the biggest impact. In other cases, you might want a more methodical process. Here's what I suggest for that.

Go through each driver below and think about whether it impacts your situation. Then look at the metrics you'd want to track to assess them. Remember that the examples I provided may be too generalized for your work. Use your industry experience to make them more specific.

Technological

- Is there something predictable about relevant technology development, at least near-term, related to your product or business? If so, what are the expected changes?

- Is there an existing "law" that helps describe the timeline for the technological change? E.g. Moore's Law and Edholm's Law. If the timeline is somewhat predictable maybe you should start working before the needed changes occur.

- Metrics: changes in pricing, processing power, electric power, and estimates for the timeline of these changes.

Social/Behavioral

- Are the required behaviors already present in niche communities? How could you learn from those niche groups?

- Where are there leading indicators of social/behavioral change? What groups influence change for the broader population?

- What enduring human behaviors are relevant?

- This driver is more difficult to predict than it seems.

Regulatory/Legal

- What relevant regulatory changes are expected? What would happen if the regulation did change? What if it did not change?

- What relevant patents will expire in the next few years?

- What relevant legal changes are expected? What influence does your organization have on that process? Who else influences that process?

Installed Base

- What is the growth in the relevant installed base? What determines that?

- What is the critical mass you need for an installed base to support your business? How does critical mass work for your business?

- Do the producers of the installed base devices and products control access in a way that would affect you?

Crisis

- Will the crisis change things temporarily? For how long?

- Will the crisis change things permanently? What other effects might we see?

- Are you coincidentally well-positioned to benefit from a specific crisis? Could you move fast enough to take advantage of the crisis? If not you, who else?

Economic

- What economic conditions favor your business?

- In which situations does economic growth or decline improve or worsen your results?

Networks

- Is there an existing network to tap into? How?

- What time and cost would it take to create or develop the needed network?

- Can you control the network?

Distribution

- What restricts current distribution? Is it speed, costs, availability, form?

- What existing demand is there that a new form of distribution would accelerate?

- What new demand could a new form of distribution generate?

Capital Access

- Is capital access in your industry scarce or plentiful? How long do you expect it to be so?

- What other industries are hot with investors? Why? How does that impact you?

- Did related industries previously give investors a bad experience? Does that impact you?

Organizational

- What types of organizations enable the product to be built effectively?

- What types of organizations demand the product?

- Would your own organizational learning enable you to move toward a sustainable business model?

Available Talent

- How fast is the talent produced? If universities are a main place of production, how many relevant graduates are produced each year?

- What are other draws for that same pool of talent? If the needed talent doesn't currently work in your industry, where do they go?

- What motivates the talent when they choose their work?

Demographic

- Is the change already present in niche communities where the demographic trend hits first?

- What do demographic charts not tell you? How does the demographics of a niche move differently from that of the whole population?

- What are the long demographic trends to build for?

- What will demographic changes do to demand?

If You Have No Strong Timing Advantage

There are times when timing is not one of your advantages.

You read about the drivers of timing, the examples, and tried the Why Now Session but then stopped. You still believe in your work, but don't think that timing is an advantage for you.

In other situations, you may have already been skeptical of the product you were pursuing. The lack of good timing just makes it easier to decline to build it.

Recognizing that you lack a timing advantage can save you from building a product you don't believe in.

You also might pause because you believe that the needed timing drivers will take too long to emerge. How to define "too long" is up to you. Should you invest now to be ready for the growth that is about to be unleashed? Or should you wait because you are still years away from the drivers converging? Let someone else go first and make mistakes as a first mover?

Where to draw that too early line is up to your perspective.

But you could decide to support what's missing in order to develop a market, confident that your business model will work later.

What if you go through the Why Now Session, build Timing Maps, and more for a series of potential products but ultimately don't come up with any strong timing advantages?

Here are some ways you could think through your options.

1. Change an element of the product.

Would changing some part of the product shift you to a new space with a timing advantage? Would you gain part of an existing niche market? Could you improve part of the business model, enabling you to make the product sustainable?

2. Extend your timing horizon.

How could you give yourself more time? Does the business model become sustainable when more time passes?

3. Search for related opportunities.

Are there lower-risk opportunities where you could gain relevant experience and then return to the original opportunity later on?

4. Change the customer you're focused on.

Changing the customer can change the value you create, what you can charge, and your costs. Are there other customer types that would be a better fit?

5. Let someone else go first.

Do you expect a lot of effort to be put into educating a new market? Are existing buyers resistant to your product?

Could you let someone else go first in order to make those mistakes for you?

6. Do it anyway and pull the future forward.

When you have companies, institutions, and individuals willing and able to devote their energy and money on something not yet possible, you can pull the future forward.

7. Recognize that timing is not the only thing. In that case, you might pursue the concept anyway.

Timing is part of the reason for success, not the only reason.

8. Give up and do something else.

There is always something else.

Bibliography

The list below comprises other thinkers, alive and dead, with whom I was able to explore this topic. And they didn't even know it.

Blank, Steven. The Four Steps to the Epiphany: Successful Strategies for Products That Win. *S.G. Blank*, [California], 2007

Fang, Irving. A History of Mass Communication: Six Information Revolutions. United States, *Taylor & Francis*, 1997.

"Founder School Session: The Future Doesn't Have to Be Incremental." YouTube, *YouTube*, 4 Apr. 2014, www.youtube.com/watch?v=gTAghAJcO1o.

Gertner, Jon. The Idea Factory: Bell Labs and the Great Age of American Innovation. United Kingdom, *Penguin Publishing Group*, 2013.

Golder, Peter N., and Gerard J. Tellis. "Pioneer Advantage: Marketing Logic or Marketing Legend?" *Journal of Marketing Research*, vol. 30, no. 2, May 1993, p. 158 - 170, https://doi.org/10.2307/3172825.

Gompers, Paul A., et al. "How Do Venture Capitalists Make Decisions?" *Journal of Financial Economics*, vol. 135, no. 1, Jan. 2020, pp. 169–190, https://doi.org/10.1016/j.jfineco.2019.06.011.

Kelly, Kevin. What Technology Wants. Germany, *Penguin Publishing Group*, 2011.

Lieberman, Marvin B., and David B. Montgomery. "First-Mover Advantages." *Strategic Management Journal*, vol. 9, no. S1, 1988, pp. 41–58, onlinelibrary.wiley.com/doi/abs/10.1002/smj.4250090706, https://doi.org/10.1002/smj.4250090706.

Lieberman, Marvin B., and David B. Montgomery. "First-Mover (Dis)Advantages: Retrospective and Link with the Resource-Based View." *Strategic Management Journal*, vol. 19, no. 12, Dec. 1998, pp. 1111–1125, https://doi.org/10.1002/(sici)1097-0266(1998120)19:12%3C1111::aid-smj21%3E3.0.co;2-w.

Lehman, Joel, and Stanley, Kenneth O. Why Greatness Cannot Be Planned: The Myth of the Objective. Germany, *Springer International Publishing*, 2015.

Morison, Elting E.. Men, Machines, and Modern Times, 50th Anniversary Edition. United States, *MIT Press*, 2016.

Noll, A. Michael. "Anatomy of a Failure: Picturephone Revisited." *Telecommunications Policy*, vol. 16, no. 4, 1 May 1992, pp. 307–316, www.sciencedirect.com/science/article/abs/pii/030859619290039R, https://doi.org/10.1016/0308-5961(92)90039-R.

Ogburn, William F., and Dorothy Thomas. "Are Inventions Inevitable? A Note on Social Evolution." *Political Science Quarterly*, vol. 37, no. 1, 1922, pp. 83–98. JSTOR, https://doi.org/10.2307/2142320.

Ridley, Matt. How Innovation Works: And Why It Flourishes in Freedom. United States, *HarperCollins*, 2020.

Simon, Herbert A. (Herbert Alexander), 1916-2001. *The New Science of Management Decision*. [1st ed.] New York: Harper, 1960.

Simonton, Dean Keith. "Independent Discovery in Science and Technology: A Closer Look at the Poisson Distribution." *Social Studies of Science*, vol. 8, no. 4, Nov. 1978, pp. 521–532, https://doi.org/10.1177/030631277800800405. Accessed 6 Apr. 2023.

Utterback, James M.. Mastering the Dynamics of Innovation: How Companies Can Seize Opportunities in the Face of Technological Change. United States, *Harvard Business School Press*, 1994.

Wagner, Andreas. Sleeping Beauties: The Mystery of Dormant Innovations in Nature and Culture. United Kingdom, *Oneworld Publications*, 2023.

Nordhaus, William D. "Do Real Output and Real Wage Measures Capture Reality? The History of Lighting Suggests Not." *RePEc: Research Papers in Economics*, 1 Jan. 1996, pp. 27–70, https://doi.org/10.7208/9780226074184-003. Accessed 27 Apr. 2023.

United States Court of Appeals for the Second Circuit. Viacom International Inc. v. YouTube, Inc., 2012.

Thank You

Many people helped me along the way toward writing this book. Especial thanks to the following readers and commenters.

Étienne Garbugli, author of *Lean B2B: Build Products Businesses Want*, invited me to present on timing to his B2B company meetup. He offered guidance and encouragement early on as I wondered if I should even pursue writing this book. Étienne's extensive comments on a draft helped set the direction I eventually took. His encouragement and check-ins over a couple years helped me stay focused on this work.

ShiaoFong Yin, my colleague at the Lloyd Greif Center for Entrepreneurial Studies at the University of Southern California, provided extensive helpful comments. She also invited me to speak on timing to her class and served as a fount of encouragement as I worked my way through the topic.

Sean Murphy, of Bootstrappers Breakfast and SKMurphy, Inc., invited me to his monthly startup workshop to present on the timing topic. In the weeks leading up to the event, Sean challenged and pushed my thinking. He was effortlessly able to recommend helpful books and relevant content.

Alex Zorychta of Not Yet Ventures originally connected on the topic of startup evaluation techniques and building supportive ecosystems. He provided helpful feedback along the way and including commenting on a draft.

Dietrich Aumann, VC at Helsana HealthInvest, provided helpful comments. He and I originally connected on the topic of evaluating startups by their unit economics, another subject I'm passionate about.

Jeffrey Broer, of Mulana VC and the University of Hong Kong, invited me to present at his startup incubator and provided encouragement and connections along the way.

Adam Berk, author of *Startup Program Design: A Practical Guide for Creating Corporate Accelerators and Incubators at Any Organization*, provided multiple connections and helped me think through value propositions while I worked through the timing topic.

Steve Forte, VC at Fresco Capital, provided helpful comments on an early draft. We originally collaborated to build startup accelerators that fit the regional needs of tech hubs outside the US, a topic where timing is relevant.

John Pollard, a past student of mine and now co-founder at Nina Protocol, provided me with thoughts and comments on an early draft. When teacher and student switch places you learn something new.

Drew Stegmaier provided helpful comments and encouragement on an early draft. He also talked through the topic with me early on as I collected my thoughts.

Joy Payton-Stevens of Frog Design read and commented on an early draft, especially providing guidance on structure.

Galen Buckwalter, of many startups, including eHarmony and psyML, helped me think through the topic over multiple lunchtime discussions. Looking forward to the next one.

Thank you to the other individuals, companies, startup accelerators, incubators, and others who contributed their thoughts and encouragement. I am grateful.

And also, thanks to SJCFEJTAGJFPRTAMDG.

Endnotes

[1] comte de Las Cases, Emmanuel-Auguste-Dieudonné, and Napoleon. Mémorial de Sainte Hélène: Journal of the Private Life and Conversations of the Emperor Napoleon at Saint Helena. United Kingdom, *H. Colburn and Company*, 1823.

[2] Wilson, Fred. "Airbnb." *AVC*, 16 Mar. 2011, avc.com/2011/03/airbnb/.

[3] Craig, Paige. "Airbnb - My Billion Dollar Lesson" *Arena VC*, July, 2015, https://arenavc.com/2015/07/airbnb-my-1-billion-lesson/

[4] Empson, Rip. "Marc Andreessen Visits Peter Thiel's Stanford Class to Talk Startups, How He Invests & the Future." *TechCrunch*, 14 May 2012, techcrunch.com/2012/05/12/marc-andreessen-visits-peter-thiels-stanford-class-to-talk-startups-how-he-invests-the-future/.

[5] "2012 Re:Invent Day 2: Fireside Chat with Jeff Bezos & Werner Vogels." YouTube, *YouTube*, 29 Nov. 2012, www.youtube.com/watch?v=O4MtQGRIIuA.

[6] United States Court of Appeals for the Second Circuit. Viacom International Inc. v. YouTube, Inc., 2012.

[7] A version of this originally appeared on my blog. "Avoid the Analysis of Others (Why Now)." *Startups Unplugged*, 15 Jan. 2023, startupsunplugged.com/why-now/avoid-the-analysis-of-others/.

[8] Stewart, Caitlin. "The Future of Virtual Reality and Augmented Reality." Market Research Blog, MarketResearch.com, 28 May 2019, blog.marketresearch.com/the-future-of-virtual-reality-and-augmented-reality.

[9] Zion Market Research. (2018, February 14). 2016 virtual reality (VR) market size revenue to grow by USD 26.89 billion in 2022. GlobeNewswire News Room. https://www.globenewswire.com/news-release/2018/02/14/1348008/0/en/2016-Virtual-Reality-VR-Market-Size-Revenue-to-Grow-by-USD-26-89-Billion-in-2022.html

[10] Intelligence, I. (n.d.). The virtual and augmented reality market will reach $162 billion by 2020. Business Insider. https://www.businessinsider.com/virtual-and-augmented-reality-markets-will-reach-162-billion-by-2020-2016-8

[11] Luke W. Graham. (2016, June 2). Why augmented reality might just outshine virtual realty. CNBC. https://www.cnbc.com/2016/06/02/why-augmented-reality-might-just-outshine-virtual-realty.html

[12] Gilbert, N. (2024, February 20). 74 virtual reality statistics you must know in 2024: Adoption, usage & market share. *Financesonline.com.* https://financesonline.com/virtual-reality-statistics/

[13]Virtual reality [VR] market size, growth, share: Report, 2030. Virtual Reality [VR] Market Size, Growth, Share | Report, 2030. (n.d.).

https://www.fortunebusinessinsights.com/industry-reports/virtual-reality-market-101378

[14] AR & VR headsets market insights. *IDC.* (n.d.). https://www.idc.com/promo/arvr

[15] Nordhaus, William D. "Do Real Output and Real Wage Measures Capture Reality? The History of Lighting Suggests Not." *RePEc: Research Papers in Economics*, 1 Jan. 1996, pp. 27–70, https://doi.org/10.7208/9780226074184-003. Accessed 27 Apr. 2023.

[16] "Founder School Session: The Future Doesn't Have to Be Incremental." *YouTube*, 4 Apr. 2014, www.youtube.com/watch?v=gTAghAJcO1o.

[17] "Founder School Session: The Future Doesn't Have to Be Incremental." *YouTube*, 4 Apr. 2014, www.youtube.com/watch?v=gTAghAJcO1o.

[18] Isaacson, Walter. *Steve Jobs*. United States, Simon & Schuster, 2013.

[19] Buffett, W. Chairman's letter - 1985. https://www.berkshirehathaway.com/letters/1985.html

[20] Golder, P. N. and G. J. Tellis (1993). "Pioneer advantage: Marketing logic or marketing legend?" Journal of Marketing Research, 30 (2), p158-170.

[21] Lieberman, Marvin B., and David B. Montgomery. "First-Mover (Dis)Advantages: Retrospective and Link with the Resource-Based View." Strategic Management Journal, vol. 19, no. 12, Dec. 1998, pp. 1111–1125

[22] Utterback, James M.. Mastering the Dynamics of Innovation: How Companies Can Seize Opportunities in the Face of Technological Change. United States, *Harvard Business School Press*, 1994.

[23] Gompers, Paul A., et al. "How Do Venture Capitalists Make Decisions?" *Journal of Financial Economics*, vol. 135, no. 1, Jan. 2020, pp. 169–190, https://doi.org/10.1016/j.jfineco.2019.06.011.

[24] Bevelin, P. (2016). All I want to know is where I'm going to die so I'll never go there: Buffett and Munger -- a study in simplicity and uncommon, common sense. *Walsworth Publishing Company*.

[25] From the "Viacom vs Google (YouTube)" lawsuit YouTube memo. United States Court of Appeals for the Second Circuit. Viacom International Inc. v. YouTube, Inc., 2012.

[26] "The Single Biggest Reason Why Start-Ups Succeed | Bill Gross | Ted." *YouTube*, 1 June 2015, www.youtube.com/watch?v=bNpx7gpSqbY&t.

[27] *Why the "Why Now" Slide Is More Important than Ever - Docsend*, www.docsend.com/blog/why-now-slide/. Accessed 15 Mar. 2024.

[28] "50 Timing Examples (the Why Now question)," *Startups Unplugged*, https://startupsunplugged.com/why-now/50-timing-examples/

[29] *Gertner, Jon. The Idea Factory: Bell Labs and the Great Age of American Innovation. United Kingdom, Penguin Publishing Group, 2013. p265*

[30] *Gertner, Jon. The Idea Factory: Bell Labs and the Great Age of American Innovation. United Kingdom, Penguin Publishing Group, 2013. p 289.*

[31] "Steve Jobs in 2010, at D8 Conference (Full Video)." *YouTube,* 8 Feb. 2015, www.youtube.com/watch?v=i5f8bqYYwps&t=256s.

[32] Damodaran, Aswath. *"Uber Isn't Worth $17 Billion."* FiveThirtyEight, FiveThirtyEight, 18 June 2014, fivethirtyeight.com/features/uber-isnt-worth-17-billion/.

[33] Gurley, Bill. *"How to Miss By a Mile: An Alternative Look at Uber's Potential Market Size."* Above the Crowd, 4 Dec. 2023, abovethecrowd.com/2014/07/11/how-to-miss-by-a-mile-an-alternative-look-at-ubers-potential-market-size/

[34] "US4131919A - Electronic Still Camera." *Google Patents*, Google, patents.google.com/patent/US4131919A/en. Accessed 15 Mar. 2024.

[35] Ridley, Matt. How Innovation Works: And Why It Flourishes in Freedom. United States, *HarperCollins*, 2020., p 171-172.

[36] Botha, Roelof. "For Media and Gaming, Virtual Reality Is the Wolf Standing Just Outside the Door." *TechCrunch*, 12 Sept. 2015, techcrunch.com/2015/09/12/for-media-and-gaming-virtual-reality-is-the-wolf-standing-just-outside-the-door/.

[37] Seltz-Axmacher, Stefan. "The End of Starsky Robotics." *Medium*, Starsky Robotics 10–4 Labs, 19 Mar. 2020, medium.com/starsky-robotics-blog/the-end-of-starsky-robotics-acb8a6a8a5f5.

[38] "Steve Jobs Secrets of Life." *YouTube*, 7 Oct. 2011, www.youtube.com/watch?v=kYfNvmF0Bqw.

[39] Quoted in the magazine *The Friend*, 1902.

[40] Ogburn, William F., and Dorothy Thomas. "Are Inventions Inevitable? A Note on Social Evolution." *Political Science Quarterly*, vol. 37, no. 1, 1922, pp. 83–98. JSTOR, https://doi.org/10.2307/2142320.

[41] Fort, Charles. *Lo!*. United States, Cosimo Classics, 2006. Originally published: 1931. p. 20.

Made in United States
Troutdale, OR
04/14/2024

19182129R00087